OBAMA IN PROPHECY

REV. DR. J. EMMETTE WEIR

Outskirts Press, Inc.
Denver, Colorado

The opinions expressed in this manuscript are solely the opinions of the author and do not represent the opinions or thoughts of the publisher. The author has represented and warranted full ownership and/or legal right to publish all the materials in this book.

Obama in Prophecy
All Rights Reserved.
Copyright © 2009 Rev. Dr. J. Emmette Weir
V2.0

Cover Photo © 2009 All rights reserved - used with permission.
Presidential hopeful Barack Obama at the Presidential Health Forum in Las Vegas, Nevada, USA, photo taken by Ralph Alswang
("Mutual respect", photo of Michelle and Barack Obama by Flickr user [http://www.flickr.com/people/myhobosoul/ My Hobo Soul] taken February 17, 2007 at the JJ Convention 2007 (Jefferson-Jackson Day fundraising event) of the Democratic Party of Virginia.

This book may not be reproduced, transmitted, or stored in whole or in part by any means, including graphic, electronic, or mechanical without the express written consent of the publisher except in the case of brief quotations embodied in critical articles and reviews.

Outskirts Press, Inc.
http://www.outskirtspress.com

ISBN PB: 978-1-4327-1233-4
ISBN HB: 978-1-4327-2350-7

Library of Congress Control Number: 2009920330

Outskirts Press and the "OP" logo are trademarks belonging to Outskirts Press, Inc.

PRINTED IN THE UNITED STATES OF AMERICA

DEDICATION

Dedicated to all "Aunt Lilys," those of the older generation,
Of all colours, nationalities, classes and creeds,
Who out of the vast treasure of their accumulated
knowledge and vivid experiences,
Passed on gems of wisdom,
To the children of this generation!

ACKNOWLEDGMENTS

St. Paul the great Apostle, writing to the Corinthians, put to them the penetrating question, "what do ye have, which ye have not received?"

The Apostle here was really urging the Corinthians to recognize the fact that each and every one of us human beings is greatly indebted to God, our Creator and those "near and dear" to us (as well as those who are not!) for whatever progress we make or whatever accomplishments we boast about, in our sojourn through this transitory life. Or, in the immortal words of John Donne:

"No man is an Island."

The profound truth of this essentially interdependent nature of us all has been very much on my mind and in my heart as I have penned the pages of "Obama In Prophecy"

Thus, I begin by thanking God, THE FATHER OF OUR SAVIOUR AND LORD JESUS THE CHRIST, WHO THROUGH HIS HOLY SPIRIT HAS GIVEN ME THE VISION AND ENDOWED ME WITH THE ABILITY TO WRITE IT.

Then, I am deeply grateful to many people, who in their own way, assisted me in getting this book "on the market."

To Ena, my dear wife of many happy years, our children, Ellsworth, Erica and Teneille, and our grand children, Jayden and Jordan, for their encouragement, "prodding" and support as this book began "to take shape" and rapidly develop.

To my siblings, Miriam, Roger and Sheila, who encouraged me and assisted by "jogging my memory" about our formative years growing up in Nassau.

To my friend Dr. Myles Munroe, who has never failed to help me.

To my long time friends, the Hon. Henry Bostwick, QC and his wife Janet Bostwick, both Bahamian icons, who over many years, have provided encouragement and practical assistance in all my literary endeavours.

To my colleagues in ministry including the Rev. Dr. Raymond Neilly, The Revs. Theophilus Rolle, Hilgrove Hamilton, Kenneth Lewis, John Stubbs and Derek C.O. Browne of the Methodist Church in the Caribbean and the Americas, Mr. Henry Knowles of the Bahamas Conference of the Methodist Church, Canon Harry Bain and the Rev. Fr. Stephen Grant of The Anglican Church, The Council and members of Our Saviour Lutheran Church in Freeport, Grand Bahama, including Dennis Lightbourne, Greg Smith, Lief Bjercke, Charlton Smith and Gena Granger for their encouraging and thought provoking comments.

To Barbara F.A. Burrows, who with enthusiastic skill and indefatigable zeal typed the manuscript, most ably assisted by the accurate editorial observations of her husband, Greg.

To the authors and publishers who granted permission to quote from their works.

To the management and staff of Outskirts press, especially my Author representative Bridget Horstmann, for sharing with me valuable information and insights, and so affording me the opportunity to share my visions and convictions with others through "Obama In Prophecy"

Yes, it is true! We all have to depend greatly upon others if we are to be faithful to the plan for our life, projected by THE GREAT ARCHITECT. That is precisely why whatever may be our achievements, there is little about which we can honestly boast!

TO GOD BE THE GLORY,
GREAT THINGS HE HATH DONE!

December, 2008 AD.
Freeport, Grand Bahama, Bahamas

CONTENTS

CHAPTER 1 1
   "THE NIGHT OLD MEN WEPT AND
   YOUNG PEOPLE (OF ALL RACES REJOICED!).

CHAPTER 2 11
   "LESSONS FROM AUNT LILY"

CHAPTER 3 21
   "PRINCES WILL COME OUT OF EGYPT"

CHAPTER 4 37
   "ETHIOPIA SHALL STRETCH OUT HER
   HANDS TO GOD"

CHAPTER 5 49
   "THE DIVINE ARCHITECT"

CHAPTER 6 63
   "YES WE CAN!"

CHAPTER 7 69
   "GO IN THE DIRECTION OF YOUR DREAMS!"

BOOK REVIEWS
   DREAMS FROM MY FATHER 85

   AUDACITY OF HOPE 93

PRAYER FOR BARACK OBAMA 97

NOTES..99

SELECT BIBLIOGRAPHY 119

CHAPTER 1
"THE NIGHT OLD BLACK MEN WEPT.......... AND YOUNG PEOPLE (OF ALL RACES!) REJOICED!"

"So" MR. OBAMA WON DER PRESIDENCY OF DER UNITED STATES! chuckled an elderly BLACK BAHAMIAN lady as she cheerfully offered her "take" on the results of the marathon, general election in which Barack Obama emerged as the first African – American President – Elect of The United States Of America. Then, "without missing a beat", she prayerfully added, "LORD JESUS!" 1

Whether the response of that old Bahamian matron, issued in context of the universal euphoria emanating from that most historic event, constituted a prayer of thanksgiving for the amazing victory of the charismatic young candidate for the Presidency; or a prayer for Divine guidance and protection for him; or a combination of both; was not clear to this writer. There can be no doubt however, that it was very much "in line" with the sentiments of many people of all colors, classes and creeds, in every corner of the globe. The meteoric ascendency of Barack Obama to the most prestigious and powerful political office in the world, is indeed vested with profound, historical, religious and theological significance!

It is not surprising therefore, that in many discussions

which took place in the wake of this earth – shattering event, people from all walks of life debated with vigor its historical and theological ramifications. 2

Thus, in the columns of the religious section of a local newspaper, a number of persons triumphantly volunteered their opinions; several of them holding tenaciously to the conviction that the election of Barack Obama to such a highly influential post could only be an act of Divine intervention.3 Again an elderly gentleman summed it up tersely:

"Rev., ' dey trow erryting against him; but God protect him!" Here it is germane to point out, that this view has not proved to be a parochial one; for people with deep religious conviction throughout the entire Caribbean, the Americas and beyond, gave expression to the belief that it was yet another manifestation of the mysterious out-working of "THE RIGHT HAND OF GOD!"4

The two SENIOR CITIZENS, both laypersons, were therefore not alone in interpreting the momentous event of November 4th 2008 AD., in terms of the concept of Divine intervention. Two prominent clergy persons, who are considerably younger and therefore representative of the present generation, have spoken along similar lines. WELL-KNOWN African-American Evangelist Bishop T.D. Jakes, in an extremely interesting and informative telecast on the eve of that historic election of Obama to the highest post in the USA, reminisced on the major changes which had taken place in race relations during his lifetime.5 Likewise the influential Anglican Priest, The Rev. Stephen Grant, Rector of the Parish of Mary Magdalene in the picturesque township of West End, Grand Bahama, expressed the very strong conviction that the LORD GOD, CREATOR AND SUSTAINER OF THE UNIVERSE orchestrated the events culminating in the election of Barack Obama as President Elect of the USA.6

Asserting that the election was essentially spiritual in nature and therefore could not be explained adequately "in the natural,"7 he declared that under normal circumstances, given the racial composition of the USA, there was "no way that Obama could be elected to serve at the helm of the world's most powerful nation."

Certainly this concept has been very much on the mind of this writer, as very early in the 21 month long electoral process and soon after Obama dramatically announced his candidacy for the presidency of the USA, I was reading the book of Genesis.8 I just could not help taking note of the striking parallels of the respective life stories of the patriarch Joseph and Obama. This biblical and theological phenomenon will be discussed in the chapters ahead. It is sufficient to note at this point, that it got me thinking about the religious and theological aspects of this event.

Coming back once more to the night of the election, it was indeed a time of tremendous historical importance. Many people who had watched the long crusade; the many ads; the debates between the youthful Barack Obama and the older veteran politician and war hero John McCain, who had touted his greater experience; the emergence of Sarah Palin and the oft quoted Joe the Plumber, rejoiced as the young Illinois senator triumphed over the honored warrior. Still there were those who wondered aloud whether Obama would win the election. On the night of Nov. 04th 2008, people in virtually every corner of the globe huddled around their televisions at home, or at special election parties in restaurants and bars to view the polling results as they were announced.

As the first results came in showing McCain in the lead, there was apprehension about the prospect of the victory of the young, audacious senator who had dared to run for the office of the President of the USA, at a time when fears that his nation appeared to be tethering on the brink of a recession bound to have repercussions in every nation on planet Earth. However, the lead of McCain soon evaporated as the results from all over America and its citizens residing abroad rapidly flooded in. It was exactly 11pm that the universally known CNN confidently predicted that Barack Obama would become the first African-American President of the USA.9

Predictably, pandemonium broke out as people everywhere rejoiced! Yes, that was a moment in time when people in every nation, from the hills of Kenya, ancestral home of the President-Elect, to the beaches of Hawaii where he was born and spent his formative years, to the halls of Chicago where he emerged as a budding young social activist, and community organizer, exulted in the momentous occasion.10 Indeed, it seemed as if the whole world was joining in the revelry as McCain conceded defeat in a most gracious speech and as President Bush sent words of congratulations, the whole world went wild with excitement! Indeed, beyond a shadow of doubt, it was one of democracy's finest hours!

Yet, not all rejoiced in the same way. There were those, notably old, black men who could remember the time when black people were subject to rigid racial segregation when they could not drink from the same water fountains, nor use the same restrooms, nor sit in the front seats of public transportation as did whites. No doubt those old men remembered when black men (no matter how old) were still called boys.11 No doubt they reflected upon the efforts of Rosa Parks, whose courageous actions led to the end of discrimination on buses and provided the impetus for Martin Luther Jr. to launch the historic Civil Rights Movement. Undoubtedly they remembered that immortal speech in Washington back in 1963, when King proclaimed " I have a dream of the time when each person will be judged, not by the color of his skin but by the content of his character" and yes, they remembered that fateful day when this young pioneer was assassinated. As they reflected on these events, the tears poured down. One of the most touching photos of election night was that of veteran social activist Rev. Jesse

Jackson who had served along with Dr. King, watching quietly with tears streaming down his cheeks.12 Contrastingly, in the midst of the energetic rejoicing of the young people of all races, there were black men of all ages who cried. Many wept with tears of joy, thanking the Almighty that he had spared their lives to see that day. They wept and while weeping, no doubt remembered their loved ones and colleagues who had fought for social justice, who had participated in the Civil Rights Movement, who had sacrificed their all in order to educate their children so that the next generation could experience a better "way of living"....... who had not lived to see this historic event. And there were old women who also wept.13 Here in the Bahamas "Mother" Gertrude Burnside, widow of prominent dentist Dr. Jackson Burnside, himself a staunch advocate of black leadership, had named their home "The White House" in anticipation of the day when a black man should set foot in the White House, not as a servant or visitor, but as "Mr. President!" 14

I was among those who could not hold back tears of emotion. I did not weep on election night, but on the following morning when President Bush prophesied that it would be a stirring sight to witness Barack Obama and his family stepping into The White House after his inauguration as the 44th President of the USA, tears streamed down.

So along with the screams of jubilation, was the contrasting flood of tears-tears of joy and thanksgiving to Almighty God for sparing our lives to see a day which so many of us did not even in our widest and wildest dreams expect to experience.

This scenario in which the old people wept while those of the younger generation rejoiced, like so much else in these happenings certainly has a striking parallel in the Bible. The reference here is to a little-known but very significant event in the history of ancient Israel. The rebuilding of the temple under the supervision of Ezra. Let me tell you about it. Back in 586BC., Israel was invaded by the Babylonians and their conquering despot, Nebuchadnezzar. These powerful enemies destroyed the walls of the city and desecrated the temple. The temple which had been built by King Solomon was the center of worship for the Israelites and as such was greatly revered. Of course the Prophets had occasion to remind them that the temple should be treated as a place of prayer and sincere worship (Jer. 7) How great then must have been their agony and deep distress as they saw the temple destroyed by their pagan foes! How they must have wept as they saw that previously magnificent building burnt to the ground by those who did not worship their God! Indeed this event must have severely devastated even the most devout amongst them. (see Psalm 73 and Psalm 81)

Later after 70 years in exile, the Persians who had since succeeded the Babylonians as the world superpower, allowed those among the Israelites who so desired, to return to their precious promised land.(Neh. 1 and 2) As a result of the efforts of Nehemiah, an able lay administrator and Ezra the priest, the walls were rebuilt and the temple restored. It is most interesting to note that the rebuilding of the temple came about as a result of the sacrificial giving of those who had returned from the exile.15

According to Holy Scripture, "When the exiles arrived at the Lord's Temple in Jerusalem, some of the leaders of the clans gave freewill offerings to help rebuild the temple on its old site. They gave as much as they could for this work and the total came to 1030 pounds of gold, 5,740 pounds of silver and robes for Priests" (Ezra2 VS. 68-69 GNB).16

What a superb example of sacrificial giving for this work of God! Then came the rededication of the Temple. What a joyous and festive event that was! There was great celebration and rejoicing by the young people, those who had been born in exile and had made the long journey back home. Amongst them also were a few members of the older generation who cherished fond memories of the magnificent temple, built by the wise King Solomon. As they saw the new temple, they were so overcome with emotion that......they wept.

As the rebuilding began, old men and women cried like babies while young men and maidens rejoiced. Therefore, as the builders laid the foundation, the Priests regaled in their shining vestments came forward with trumpets, as did the Levites and the musically gifted sons of Asaph "and they sang responsively, praising and giving thanks to the Lord." "For He is good, for His steadfast love endures forever towards Israel" and all the people shouted with a great shout when they praised the Lord because the foundation of the house of the Lord was laid.

But many of the Priests and Levites and heads of Fathers' houses, old men who had seen the first house, wept with a loud voice when they saw the foundation of this house being laid, though many shouted for joy, so that the people could not distinguish the sound of the joyful shout from the sound of the people's weeping, for the people shouted with a great shout and the sound was heard afar" (Ezra 3 Vs 11-13 RSV).

According to the Good Book then, the mixture of emotions was such, that the rejoicing of the young could not be distinguished from the weeping of the aged.

Nor did one drown out the other; rather they joined together in a crescendo of praise and thanksgiving to Almighty God, for the privilege of being there, not only to witness, but also to participate in the rebuilding of the temple to the glory of God.

What then can we say about the election of Obama as the first African American President of the USA? Is it an example of Divine intervention or just lucky coincidence? What lessons can we learn from this event? These are the questions with which we shall grapple in the chapters of this contribution.

Read on and come to your own conclusions. Whether you agree with the old lady who exclaimed "Lord Jesus!" and the others who hold to a similar theological position, or just regard it as a purely secular event having nothing to do with Religion or Theology, it is hoped that you will indeed benefit in some positive way from reading "Obama In Prophecy."

MISS LILLIAN WEIR
"AUNT LILY"

CHAPTER 2
"LESSONS FROM AUNT LILY"

I was born on Friday, May 14 1937 at the Bahamas General Hospital in Nassau, Bahamas. At eight o clock in the evening! Being the eldest of the four children of the late Gaspar Emmett Weir, well-known Land Surveyor, and Eunice Jeanette Weir nee Taylor, eminent Bahamian educator, our parents, faithful members of Wesley Methodist Church, Grants Town sought to bring up their children "in the nurture and admonition of the Lord", in accord with the Baptismal vows of the Church.1 Thus , my siblings (Miriam, Roger, Sheila) and I, attended "Church and Sunday School" as often as three times every Sunday, walking all the way from and to our home, taking it "in our stride" to cover a total distance of about three to four miles by foot! Indeed, sometimes my brother delighted "to trot" the whole round trip." As children, growing up in the forties and early fifties in a small, tightly knit community, we walked not only to Church and Sunday School on Sundays but also "to school" on week days!

Besides our parents however, there were a number of aunts who helped to raise us. Those were certainly the days of the extended family and all adults in the community took it upon themselves to discipline all the children.

Indeed most Bahamian families at that time lived by the old African adage: "It takes a village to raise a child".

Amongst "Aunts" (virtually all adult lady friends were called "Aunt"), there can be no doubt that the most influential was "Aunt Lily.") A music teacher by profession, she gave many musicians their "start". A devout Christian, she served as Sunday School Superintendent at Wesley Sunday school. Besides teaching music however, she imparted gems of wisdom based on years of experience to all young people who came under her magnetic influence!

When going out to work, or attending a church service or public meeting of any kind, our parents would often leave us at Aunt Lily, quite confident that we were in "good hands." She had a big yard on Baillou Hill Road and Meeting Street. It was a delight to play in the yard especially during the summer when scarlet plums, dillies (sapodillas) and "conneps" (guineps) were in season!

IN ADDITION TO THE PROFOUND, INCIPIENT INFLUENCE OF PARENTAL CARE, THE SOURCES OF OUR UPBRINGING IN THOSE FORMATIVE YEARS WERE:

1. The academic lessons we received at school during the week.
2. The lessons in moral and spiritual values received in Sunday School.
3. The lessons for living imparted to us by "Aunt Lily".

Yes, whether in Sunday School on the first day of the week or at her home during the week, we were constantly with "Aunt Lily." Bear with me then as I share with you some important lessons from "Aunt Lily". I truly believe that you will find them both very interesting and useful, and most of all quite illuminating in a study of the religious and theological significance of the life and witness of BARACK OBAMA.

First, it is of fundamental importance to emphasize, that as a disciplinarian "from the old school" Aunt Lily insisted on punctuality! It is often observed humorously people of the African Diaspora that they tend to be late.2

Reference is made accordingly in the Southern states of The USA to "CPT" (COLOURED PEOPLE'S TIME).

In the Bahamas, it is known as "Bahamian Time". Whilst a student in Jamaica, back in the early seventies, I recall that there was a popular play with the title" Eight O, Clock Jamaica time, starting 8:30!"

Of course, "Aunt Lily", had zero tolerance for this lackadaisical attitude toward time.3 Rather, she insisted that everything be done on time; holding tenaciously to the teaching of the book of Ecclesiastes, "For everything there is time and everything a season under the sun."4 Thus, she expected us to plan each day, beginning with devotions and breakfast at 8:00am. Up until this day, having served in Ministry for many years and passed retirement age, I still feel somewhat guilty when I eat breakfast after 8:00am. Yes, after eight, it does seem late!

"Aunt Lily" then, was a woman of principle! It is pertinent to note here, that one of the principles that she insisted upon was the making of New Year's resolutions. She urged her students to make resolutions at the beginning of the New Year, and even gave them hints on how to keep those self determined commitments. Indeed, Aunt Lily was never, ever lacking in advice when resolutions were "being done".5

She thus, urged that we should realize the priority of making resolutions; for she uncompromisingly believed that the setting of definite goals at specific times was the key to success in life!

In this regard she was quick to warn that "Life is no bed of roses!" Indeed, she pointed out, that in our sojourn through this transitory life, there were bound to be times when we would suffer failure, experience frustration and meet defeat! What should our response be when we encounter such bitter experiences?

Well, Aunt Lily would advise us to acknowledge our failures, tackle them "head on", forget them and try to do better next time. To be concise, this great Bahamian matron of yesteryear would agree with Rudyard Kipling, that you can "make it" in your struggles and endeavours. "If you can meet with triumph and disaster and treat both those imposters just the same."

According to "Aunt Lily" then, it is not acceptable to "give up" or become despondent when we encounter setbacks in life.

Nor must we fall into the debilitating self-deception that we could do no better! Rather we must dry our tears, "pick up the pieces", engage in self- help and move on; dreaming new dreams, setting new goals, aiming for new heights! As such, she certainly was in accord with that great African-American educator, the late Benjamin E. Mays, mentor of Martin Luther King Jr. in boldly asserting that: -"Failure to reach one's goal is not the great tragedy of life. The great tragedy of life is having no goal to reach!" 6

Here, it is useful to point out that Aunt Lily urged us to be realistic in making decisions about our goals. You see, too often people set out a long list of goals that they would like to achieve, and just as often they fail to achieve them. Nothing is more devastating to one's self esteem than constant failure! Thus it is better to set a few well - defined goals which may be realistically achieved than to make a long list of goals which just "might not get done".

Continuing in this vein, "Aunt Lily" taught us that persistence is absolutely essential if we are to meet our immediate commitments and attain our long-term goals. She never got tired of speaking to us about the dignity of honest labour, industry and perseverance. She encouraged us to always try to be the best that we can be. She was not alone in calling upon the younger generation to exercise persistence.

I vividly recall while researching for my PhD in Scotland back in the late seventies, that my study roommate was an African student named Daniel Antwi who hailed from Ghana.7 Whenever I became discouraged or was "down in the dumps" in the course of those very demanding studies, (made worse by those long, cold months of the Scottish winter!), he would encourage me by telling about a former headmaster. Yes, that African educator always urged his students to; "Keep at it! Never give in to defeat! Keep at it!!!!!!!!). Just the thought of that African teacher so vibrantly encouraging his students, inevitably lifted my spirits and I resumed my studies with renewed determination to attain my academic goal.

Now, "Aunt Lily" was nurtured and developed into a fine Christian young lady and spent most of her adult life at a time when there was a strong, if at times subtle element of racial tension between the two main racial groups. Whereas blacks or "coloured people " comprised the majority of the population, both economic and political power were wielded by a white oligarchy, known as the "The Bay Street Boys." In those days before the coming of "majority rule," Bahamian blacks were second class citizens in their own country. 8

Growing up in such an oppressive atmosphere, one might have expected "Aunt Lily" to harbour an attitude of resentment, if not antipathy towards white Bahamians. But she did not.

That was not "Aunt Lily's" way of dealing with racism. While certainly sympathizing and even silently supporting those engaged in the struggle for social justice "for the people", she never engaged in condemnation of white Bahamians.9 On the contrary, while demonstrating obvious pride in being black. she held tenaciously to the bedrock of this pride, without exercising prejudice toward her white Bahamian contemporaries. Thus, by emphasizing the cardinal virtues cited above, "Aunt Lily" exhorted her students to so develop their talents, that they would eventually attain economic parity with the whites. As a child of her time, she did not place high priority on socializing with whites; only on being equal to them.

A lesson to be learned from Aunt Lily is certainly the fact that it is possible to develop pride in one's race, without developing prejudice towards others. As indicated, Aunt Lily certainly had great pride in being black. Whenever she received reports of progress on the part of black leaders, whether in the United States or at home, she rejoiced greatly. Like most black Bahamians she was well-versed in the Bible. A favourite text, giving support to her pride in the achievement of blacks was taken from Psalm 68" the Black man's Psalm: "Princes will come out of Egypt; Ethiopia will stretch out her hands to God!" Psalm 68: 31, AV. 10

Even now after more than a half- century, I can still picture her reading the newspaper or listening to the news, repeating with obvious relish and anticipation the words of that same prophetic Psalm, whenever she learnt of some achievement by black persons.

Aunt Lily found great encouragement and hope in this seminal Biblical text. While not satisfied with the oppressive conditions of blacks in the United States and her own country, she drew inspiration from this passage, believing that the time would eventually come when oppressed black people would emerge to attain equality and prosperity. Not concerned with the complexities of textual research or philology, Aunt Lily interpreted this text, in the language of scholarship- eschatology i.e., that in the long run, black people will triumph over their oppressions. Yes, this text inspired Aunt Lily to anticipate the time when in the words of the late Martin Luther King Jr. "A person would be judged, not by the colour of his skin, but the content of his character" 11

An emphasis on punctuality… determination to succeed… the dignity of labour… self-help… persistence…

pride in one's race without prejudice towards others.

Hm! Hmm! Hmm!! Hmmm!!! Was there one prominent African-American leader of yesteryear who strongly advocated and indeed epitomized these virtues? THE ANSWER IS AT HAND... NONE OTHER THAN BOOKER TALLAFERRO WASHINGTON (1856-1915).

Yes, this eminent US Negro leader, who rose from slavery to study at Hampton Normal and Agricultural Institute in Virginia to establish Tuskegee Normal and Industrial institute in Alabama, proved to be a great source of encouragement to many blacks during the turbulent years of their upward mobility in an era of bitter racial segregation. As one authority points out "To many Americans at the turn of the 20th century, Booker T. Washington symbolized the desire of blacks to rise to self improvement..." 12

In a sense, it is extremely instructive to trace the historical process whereby the influence of Booker T. Washington (no one ever pronounced his second name, always using the initial "T") was brought to bear upon black Bahamian families, such as the Eneas and Burnside clans, and mine, the Weirs. It came about as a result of the fact that a considerable number of ambitious black Bahamians were educated at Historically Black Institutions of tertiary education, including those associated with, or operated in accord with the principles espoused by Booker T. Washington.

Amongst those pioneers in the field of education was my great-uncle, Charles Hilton Weir, who was an enthusiastic, unashamed admirer of this great African - American educator.13 In his small, home library there were many of the works of Mr. Washington, with pride of place being his magnum opus, "Up From Slavery!" It is not surprising therefore, to note that upon his return home to the Bahamas, he sought to impart to all members of his family the virtues emphasized by "Booker T." Included were his nephew, my father Gaspar Emmett Weir and of course his sister Lillian Weir, whom both we and the black Bahamian community at - large affectionately called "Aunt Lily." So, in a manner most mysterious, which can only be recognized as another manifestation of the working of the "right hand of God, the principles taught by Booker T. Washington impacted the character development of my siblings and me, contributing in a manner most profound, to whatever successes we have attained in our sojourn through this transitory life.14

What does all this have to do with the life and times of Barack Hussein Obama? Well, just fast-track from the days of Booker T. Washington to the present……. specifically Friday November 07 2008…. just three days after that historic night. Black men cried and young people (of all races) REJOICED!

Yes, three eventful days of universal rejoicing had transpired since Obama became the first African-American to be elected President of the United States. At that time, when the whole world hailed his victory at the polls; in the midst of the revelry there was deeply ingrained fear in the hearts of many, that the world may sink into an economic slump reminiscent of The Great Depression of the 1920's. At this time when finances "were low," but expectations high, the whole world waited with bated breath and tense anticipation for his first major press conference after his triumph at the polls.

Speaking with the dignity and the sense of responsibility commensurate with the status of one elected to the most powerful post on planet Earth, the young charismatic leader emphasized the need for fiscal discipline, hard work, realism and perseverance…… just the virtues advocated by Booker T. Washington many decades earlier. Having already warned the American public that "our climb will be steep", he reiterated this message based on a credential ethical posture, declaring that "Some of the choices that we're going to make are going to be difficult." Such a realistic approach is clearly what was needed and what the nation had to hear! Appropriately he admonished, "It is not going to be quick. It's not going to be easy for us to dig ourselves out of the hole that we are in."15 There can be no doubt that in voicing such sentiments in his opening salvo, Barack Obama was at one with Booker T. Washington!

This is not to suggest that Barack Obama was simply regurgitating the ideas of Booker T. Washington. It is asserted however, that there is much in common between these two black leaders.

Incidentally, it is most interesting to note that although described as "Black" or "African-American", both came from a mixed racial background. Whereas the parents of Booker T. Washington were a white man and a slave girl, Barack's father was a black man who hailed from Kenya in East Africa and his mother was a white middle class American who prized a good education. 16

In this regard, it is noteworthy to bear in mind, that neither Booker T. Washington nor Barack Obama demonstrated the strong antipathy towards white people that has characterized the approach of the militant members of the Civil Rights Movement, or other groups such as the Black Muslims and the Black Panthers. Can it be that these men's more liberal approach to white people has something to do with their mixed racial background? This and other related questions will be addressed later in our discussion.

Meanwhile, let us ponder further Aunt Lily's favorite text -: "PRINCES WILL COME OUT OF EGYPT; ETHIOPIA WILL STRETCH OUT HER HANDS TO GOD" 17

Who are the princes who will come out of Egypt? What will motivate them in their exploits? What is the meaning of Ethiopia in this text, anyhow? More poignantly, was Aunt Lily correct in her interpretation and application of it?

These and other related questions pertaining to black leadership will challenge our minds in the chapters ahead. Stay tuned!

"NOW THEREFORE BE NOT GRIEVED,
NOR ANGRY WITH YOURSELVES,
THAT YE SOLD ME HITHER:
FOR GOD DID SEND ME
BEFORE YOU TO PRESERVE LIFE"
GENESIS 45:5

CHAPTER 3
"PRINCES WILL COME OUT OF EGYPT"

WE LIVE IN A WORLD OF EXTREMELY RAPID CHANGE AND INSTANT ACTION! Jets, flying through the atmosphere at supersonic speeds, whisk their anxious passengers to their destinations, covering in hours, distances which took our ancestors days, weeks even months to reach. In the area of communications, we contact others by means of telephone, facsimile and e-mail almost instantly, expecting a reply right away, instead of waiting for days and even weeks for replies by mail as our fore-fathers did. Indeed, we have become so accustomed to speedy action in this "microwave generation"1 that a computer which takes more than a few seconds to respond when we press "the mouse" is deemed slow!!!!!!!!!!

"RUSH!" "DEAD-LINE!" "TOP PRIORITY!" "URGENT!" these are the watch-words of the age in which "we live" and changes predicted by Alvin Toffler in his epochal bestseller" Future Shock" nearly a generation ago, have already "come to pass" (to use a popular Biblical expression!)2 or, as a young Caribbean churchman graphically put it, "when 'now' has passed; it never comes back!" 3

The rapid changes evident in the field of technology, are also reflected in the realms of the socio-economic, political and international affairs. This writer certainly recalls the time when many nations which are now independent, in charge of their own local and international causes (including his own, the Commonwealth of the Bahamas) were colonies, controlled by the powerful colonial "Mother Countries" of the North Atlantic.4

Turning to that aspect of human behavior known as "race relations", the changes that have taken place in recent years, have proved to be nothing less than outstanding!.

For instance, not many years ago, a white American sports enthusiast, short sightedly (albeit confidently!) asserted, "Golfers will always be white and caddies will always be black!"5 little did he realize, even in his wildest dreams, that not long after his passing, TIGER WOODS would emerge as the greatest golfer of all times!!!

When early in the year 2007 a young energetic African – American senator from Illinois "with a funny name", launched his ambitious campaign for the nomination of the Democratic Party as it's candidate for the Presidency of the USA, comparatively few persons outside his own constituency knew him, and fewer knew what to make of him! 6 Yet those who did, were deeply impressed by his charismatic, magnetic personality, being absolutely convinced that he had "what it takes" to serve in the world's most powerful political office.7 As he made rapid progress, drawing thousands of eager supporters with the rallying cry, "YES WE CAN", defeating powerful rivals of both major American political parties, the whole world took note and realized that he was indeed a serious candidate for the very prestigious post. Well do I remember watching a TV newscast in which a young white American, who having met him excitedly shouted, " I shook hands with a future President of the USA! Yes, when so many persons from all races supported Obama, it was evident that a new age had dawned in the area of race relations. That's precisely why, as we have seen, when at 11 pm on November 4., 2008, CNN predicted that Barack Obama had clinched the victory in the race for the White House, old black men who never dreamed that they would live to see the day when a Black Man was elected to enter "The White House" as "Mr. President", just ... wept! 8

There can be no doubt that the extremely rapid rise of Barack Obama to the pinnacle of political power "in the world today" is certainly in keeping with the spirit of change characteristic of the "microwave generation." Indeed, it can be asserted, without fear of challenge, that there are very few instances of such a rapid rise to prominence in the highly competitive world of political activity. There is however, a sterling example of comparable rapid promotion to political power of a person who belonged to a "minority group" in the Bible – the meteoric ascendency of Joseph, the Hebrew servant to rule as viceroy of Pharaoh in ancient Egypt. Indeed, so striking are the parallels between the ancient Israelite and the contemporary African – American that this matter definitely merits study at much greater depth.'

Here, it is germane to point out that the people of the African Diaspora in the Americas and the Caribbean have traditionally drawn inspiration from Holy Scripture, especially the Exodus account of the Old Testament, in their struggles for social and political justice. Thus in Negro spirituals such as "Go down Moses" and the modern Caribbean song, " The Right Hand Of God", they have expressed their yearning for freedom by turning to the struggle of the Israelites for liberation from Egypt, their house of bondage. (Exodus 1-15). It is not surprising therefore, that certain of the leaders of the people of the Southern United States and the Caribbean have been compared to characters drawn from the Exodus experience of Israel.9 Thus, many Blacks during the Civil Rights Movement spoke of Martin Luther King as "Moses." Likewise many engaged in the struggle for Majority Rule and later, Independence, referred to Sir Lynden Pindling, the moving spirit behind these major political developments in the Bahamas, as "Moses."10 Moreover, while serving in Jamaica back in the early seventies, I recall an election campaign in which the late Rt. Hon. Michael Manley was referred to as "Joshua."

Now, it is quite significant to point out that in all the political campaigns cited, the people have drawn inspiration from the Exodus-Sinai tradition of the Hexateuch, the first six books of the Bible. However, as already indicated, when it comes to Barack Obama, there is another Biblical paradigm which is relevant- the Joseph tradition of Genesis. Indeed, as indicated, there are striking parallels between Joseph and Obama. In both we see one who comes from a minority group to attain prominence in a great and influential nation – one in Egypt, the greatest nation of antiquity, the other in the United States, the most powerful nation in the world today. It is submitted therefore, that when one reflects profoundly upon the life and rapid political progress of Barack Obama, the Biblical character who most readily comes to mind is ..... JOSEPH. We proceed then, by examining the relevant Biblical passages about Joseph the Patriarch, drawing comparisons along the way, with Barack Obama.

Here, it is most important to bear in mind the unique theological and literary character of the Joseph Narrative – Genesis 37, 39 – 50. Eminent German scholar, the late Gerhard von Rad, 11 universally recognized as one of the great authorities of the twentieth century on the Theology of the Old Testament, embarks upon his study of it thus:

"We begin with a brief word about the literary quality of the Joseph story as a whole. It is distinct from all previous narratives because of its unusual length, for it considerably exceeds the length of the longest of the patriarchal stories, the one about Eleizer's suit of Rebekah (chp. 24). Further, it has not attained this length by means of a gradual comprehensive composition of individual narrative units. It does not belong to an epic cycle, but it is from beginning to end an organically constructed narrative, no single segment of which can have existed independently as a separate element of tradition." 12

One only has to read the chapters of Genesis which comprise the Joseph narrative to realize that what the scholar has to say is most illuminating. For, with the exception of chapter 38, the whole narrative moves with a freshness and fluidity indicating that the writer, under divine inspiration, weaves his theology into the fabric of a most interesting story of how a young Hebrew, a member of a minority group, rises to prominence in Egypt. Indeed as will be demonstrated, the many and varied events of his life demonstrate the operation of THE RIGHT HAND OF GOD.

The story of Joseph with its "ups and downs", beginning from his boyhood, when as the favorite son of Jacob, he was given "the coat of many colors" and as a dreamer, incurred the wrath of his jealous brothers, who sold him into servanthood in Egypt, to his most eventful ascent to become administrative ruler of Egypt is well documented in "the Joseph narrative." As his career is summed up in a certain translation, "The Lord loved Joseph and he was a lucky fellow."13 The Joseph narrative, then, may be summarized thus:

THE JOSEPH NARRATIVE (SUMMARY)

GENESIS
Chap. 37
"Joseph the Dreamer," loved by doting father. Hated by jealous siblings. Beaten, thrown into a pit, rescued and sold to merchants going down to Egypt. (talk about "sibling rivalry!")

Genesis
39 Promoted to manager of Potiphar's household.

Wrongly accused of sexual advances by Potiphar's wife.

Thrown into prison.

40. Interpreted dreams of Pharaoh's butler, who was restored to his post, and his baker, who was executed!

41. Successfully interpreted two dreams of Pharaoh, and rapidly promoted to Pharaoh's viceroy, CEO of Egypt.

42. Jacob sends Joseph's brothers to Egypt to buy grain.

43. The brothers return to Canaan and when their food supplies get low, they return to Egypt.

44. The missing cup found in BENJAMIN'S sack.

45. Joseph reveals himself to his brethren

46. Jacob departs for Egypt.

47. Jacob and his family ("The children of Israel") reside in Goshen.

48. Jacob blesses the sons of Joseph.

49. Jacob blesses all his sons.

50. End of the Joseph Narrative.

The account of the rise of Joseph to power in Egypt can only be appreciated by realizing the social status of the Hebrews nearly two thousand years before the birth of Christ. The "Hebrews" as several scholars have pointed out were a nomadic people, who made their living by the herding of cattle, sheep and goats. 14 They travelled throughout the Ancient Middle East, seeking pasture for their animals. As such, they were despised by the Egyptians, whose much more highly developed civilization was based on agriculture. The Nile River, with its well watered and fertile banks, provided the basis for it's agrarian economy and highly developed 'life style' compared to the more rustic customs of their nomadic contemporaries!

THE Hebrews then, were a despised minority group, nomads who visited this more developed country in times of famine to benefit from the more prosperous, agrarian economy of one of the world's earliest civilizations, which had been in existence many centuries before the coming of Joseph and his entourage.

Again, von Rad has a useful contribution to make. Taking issue with the traditional assumption that "Hebrew" was originally a tribal designation, he declares:

"Hebrews seem rather to have been a fluctuating lower level of the population who, without possession and perhaps also tribal affiliation, must have been a danger for those states. 'Hebrew' is thus a designation that originally said nothing about what national group a person belonged to, but rather told something about his social and legal status." 15

The scholar goes on to demonstrate that the term "Hebrew" later applied to all Israelites (Literally "the children of Israel ie. Jacob.) But, at the time of Joseph (c. 1800 BC), the Hebrews were a wandering group of nomads, condescendingly "looked down upon" by the settled, more prosperous and sophisticated Egyptians.

THE PROMOTION, THEN OF A HEBREW TO THE TOP POST IN EGYPT, NEXT ONLY TO THE NOR-

MALLY ALL- POWERFUL PHARAOH, WOULD HAVE CONSTITUTED AN EVENT OF TREMENDOUS SIGNIFICANCE WITH MAJOR SOCIAL AND POLITICAL RAMIFICATIONS. IT WOULD INDEED, HAVE BEEN NOTHING LESS THAN"BREAKING NEWS."

NO DOUBT, THE AVERAGE EGYPTIAN "ON THE STREET" WOULD HAVE CERTAINLY TAKEN NOTE OF SUCH AN UNPRECEDENTED EVENT, SURELY COMPARABLE TO THE ELECTION OF AN AFRICAN – AMERICAN TO THE TOP POST IN THE UNITED STATES TODAY.

Is it then, too fanciful to imagine how such an event would have been handled had the ancients been privileged to use the mass media of communications available to us as a result of modern technology? I think not!

"THE EGYPTIAN TIMES"

"The recent appointment of a young Hebrew to the top 16 administrative post in our nation by Pharaoh is certainly a very significant event. Indeed, it is unprecedented in the long history of our highly developed nation. It is a real recognition of his great administrative ability that he should be appointed to a position of such prestige and power at the comparatively young age of thirty.

The meteoric rise of Zaphenath – paneah 17 to political prominence is more remarkable not only because he belongs to a minority group, but also because it has not been without blemish. (According to confirmed reports, he was thrown into prison as a result of a sex scandal involving his boss' wife!). There can be no doubt however, that he has been promoted because of his ability to interpret dreams, his proven administrative skills, his wise counsel and general charisma, causing many, including Pharaoh, to place great confidence in him.

Looking towards the future, it will not be long before the reputed administrative skills of the young Hebrew will be put to the test. While there has been a measure of prosperity in recent years, economists predict that there may be a down turn in the economic sphere during the years ahead. Climatic changes may result in a reduced amount of rainfall, which would affect the flow of water in the Nile River. Should that happen, the years of prosperity which we have been experiencing can well turn into years of famine and even may cause a recession. It will be extremely interesting to see how the newly appointed viceroy will deal with these economic challenges.

It is of course expected, that his appointment will lead to improved relationships between the citizens of our nation and minority groups such as the Hebrews. Anything which can be done to improve these relationships merits careful attention. Our prayers and best wishes are extended to the young Hebrew as he assumes this powerful post as Pharaoh's viceroy." 18

It is submitted that this imaginary ancient Egyptian news report, certainly enabled us to focus upon, in a manner most graphic, the striking parallels between the ancient Israelite patriarch JOSEPH and the contemporary African – American political luminary BARACK OBAMA.

As has been pointed out, both emerged from the ranks of minority groups to attain positions of great authority in a remarkably short period. Both have proved to be gifted as charismatic leaders in whom others naturally placed great trust. Thus, the rise of Joseph to power in Egypt was possible not only because he was favored by Pharaoh, but also because he was readily accepted by the Egyptians. (Gen.45). Likewise, in his rise to power, Barack Obama received the enthusiastic support of both Black and White voters, As such, both Joseph, who married an Egyptian woman, and Barack whose father was black and his mother white, can be described as "bridge personalities", naturally able to cross the racial divide and bring people of different racial and social backgrounds together. Moreover, both proved to be persons endowed with physical agility as well as mental ability, courage and propensity" to grasp the opportunity." Thus Joseph as he spoke to the Pharaoh gave him sound advice, resulting in his meteoric rise to authority, and Barack Obama, in making his famous debut speech at the Democratic National Convention in 2004 both demonstrated how utterly important it is for the alert individual to grasp opportunities for advancement when they come his/her way.

Of course it is realized that there always exists the danger of pushing an analogy too far when comparing the contributions of any two persons. So, it is not the intention here to seek to suggest an exact parallel in every minute detail between the life of the ancient Israelite patriarch and the contemporary African-American politician. Obviously that is untenable. For instance, to the best knowledge and belief of this writer, no sex scandal (alleged or real!) has tarnished the career of Barack Obama, in contrast to that of Joseph and indeed, many other leaders, political and religious, ever since the palmy days of the Pharaohs to the present.

Nevertheless, it is possible to pinpoint yet another striking parallel between the respective contributions of the two outstanding personalities under discussion here. It has transpired that both came to power at a time of severe economic crises! In Egypt, it was the "seven years of famine" (Genesis 41: 25-27, 54-57). In the case of the United States, it is recognized that the great nation is facing the most formidable challenge to its economic buoyancy since the Great Depression of the early twentieth century. Obama then, comes to serve as President precisely at a time, when great hopes are vested with regard to his expected ability to solve the economic challenges of the USA. Leaders in various fields of economic endeavor from the banks, auto industry and commerce have expressed as much. Indeed, the words of Mordecai to his niece Esther in a time of political crisis in ancient Israel, may be applied with equal poignancy to Barack Obama, "And who knows whether thou art come to the kingdom for such a time as this." 19

It is clear in reading the Bible, that two major challenges faced Joseph when he assumed the highest administrative post in ancient Egypt – dealing with the economic crisis ("the seven years of famine") and improving the social status of the Hebrews. According to "The Joseph Narrative, he succeeded admirably in dealing with these challenges, taking stringent measures to deal with the economic viability of Egypt and ensuring that his people were given a place of refuge in Egypt, where they remained for more than four centuries, until the coming of a new Pharaoh, "who knew not Joseph." At that time, a new dynasty emerged in that ancient land, which was hostile to the Hebrews, and the oppressive measures culminated in the Exodus, their rescue from "their house of bondage" under the leadership of Moses, servant of THE LORD.20

In keeping with our observations thus far, the challenges facing Barack Obama as he assumes the office of President of the United States of America are strikingly similar – to deal immediately and decisively with the "struggling economy" of the nation, and certainly to make a positive difference in the complex field of race relations.

As we have already seen, high hopes for his success in tackling the steep challenges in "turning around" the economy are held by people from all walks of life. But what about race relations? What is expected of him in this most complex area of human behavior? Considering the long history of race relations in the USA with it's "ups and downs" from the days of slavery, to the Civil War, Reconstruction and the Civil Rights Movement under Dr. Martin Luther King Jr., there can be no doubt that it emerges as a matter of top priority as Barack Obama assumes the Presidency of the USA.

By an appeal to the imagination, we have speculated as to how the media of ancient Egypt might have responded to Pharaoh's appointment of the Hebrew Joseph to the post of supreme administrative responsibility. It is, therefore, quite justifiable and appropriate, to draw attention to what a contemporary journal has to say about Barack Obama, with regard to the matter under consideration here. In its editorial, published the morning after Barack Obama's election, under the provocative headline, "What a black President will mean for race relations." It was observed that:

"By everyone's measure, the election of an African – American President just four decades after race riots marked the tumultuous end of segregation is extraordinary. As Barack Obama noted in his victory speech Tuesday night, it is a measure of the nation's ability to reinvent itself as it strives to attain the elusive American ideal. But what will Obama's presidency mean for race relations going forward? Is it possible that the country is moving into the "post- racial" era?

It certainly will not mean a quick end to bigotry. Campaign interviews over the pre-election months unearthed plentiful stories of racist attitudes. In the South, John McCain got twice as many white votes as Obama did." 21

THE WRITER, THEN GOES ON TO MAKE THE POINT THAT THE ELECTION OF OBAMA WOULD NOT SUDDENLY BRING A SOLUTION TO THE ENDEMIC PROBLEMS OF THE BLACK POPULATION CAUSED BY A HIGH RATE OF UNEMPLOYMENT, THE DECLINE IN HOME AND FAMILY LIFE, AND A HIGH INCIDENCE OF CRIME.

Or, to put it another way, the appointment of the first African- American President will not prove to be "a magic wand" which will suddenly transform the state of African–

Americans overnight. Yet, there can be no doubt that his assumption to this office has already exerted a very positive effect upon the younger generation of African–Americans. There can be no doubt that the election of Obama is proving a source of pride and inspiration on the part of many.22

Here it is relevant to point out that, in the process of writing his first book, "Dreams From My Father," Obama relates an experience which foreshadowed the crucial role that he was destined to carry out with regard to race relations. It occurred late at night (or in the early hours of the morning!) when, as a young social worker he was discussing with a young woman his vision for the advancement of blacks not only of the USA, but of all nations. She reprimanded him in such a manner that it made him feel "like I was somehow responsible for the fate of the entire black race." 23 Little did that young progressive white lady realize that her comment would prove to be nothing other than prophetic. For, as Barack Obama assumes the Office of President of the United States, the world's most prestigious and powerful political office, there can be no doubt that the eyes of black people "in every corner of the globe" are, and will continue to be focused upon him. It has been the impression of this writer, that in the crucial months of campaigning for this office, that in a manner most profound, the destiny of every Black person on planet Earth was somehow bound up with that of the young charismatic African – American candidate for the Presidency of the United States of America.

Thus far, our concentration from a Biblical perspective, has been on the Joseph Narrative of Genesis. We come now to consider another text which is relevant to our study: To whit:

"Princes will come out of Egypt;
Ethiopia will stretch out her hands to God."
Ps. 68:31

As we have seen, this was one of Aunt Lily's favorite texts, quoted whenever a Black person made advances, especially in the political arena.24 Indeed, it has proved to be a favorite text of many Movements which have touted the ascendancy of those who belong to the African Diaspora. It was the main Biblical text of the Back to Africa Movement led by Marcus Garvey, which drew strong support in both the Southern USA and the Caribbean.25

This text, from the perspective of "Black Exegesis," has been interpreted to refer to the ascendency of Black People to political and religious leadership. Since Obama has emerged as the first African- American President of the USA, it may appropriately be applied to him. It is however, essential to bear in mind that many leaders in the past suffered and gave of their best in order to bring about racial equality in the USA. Indeed, going back to the days of slavery, when there were those who revolted against servitude, to the era of Emancipation and the Reconstruction, to the Civil Rights Movement of the middle of the twentieth century, there have been those of African descent who have championed the cause of the oppressed.26 Included in this number then must be the early pioneers who sought full freedom and equality; leaders such as Nat Turner, Marcus Garvey, Martin Luther King Jr., The Rev. Jesse Jackson, The Rev. Joseph Lowrey, Julian Bond and a host of others, far too numerous to be named here. They fought, struggled and labored so that the time would come when a Black Man would set foot in "the White House," not as a servant or visitor, but as "Mr. President." That is why so many old men wept at 11pm on November 4, in the year of our Lord two thousand and eight! 27

To the "Princes who came out of Africa" we should add Booker T. Washington. For, as we have noted, there are most interesting parallels to be discerned in comparing the respective contributions of that African - American leader of the early twentieth century and that of the Senator from

Illinois, now the President. Notably, neither of them demonstrated a strong antipathy towards Caucasians. Indeed, both were criticized by the more militant groups for their charitable attitude to whites, as is well documented. 28

A significant difference between the respective approaches of Washington and Obama however, emerges upon more careful examination. You see, Washington believed that through "hard work, thrift and self-help Negroes would improve their status and would ultimately win acceptance by whites." 29 His thinking was dominated by the concept of "separate but equal" and in this regard, he was "a child of his times." 30 Obama, however, went a bold step further, rejecting any idea of inferiority or of "having to be accepted by the white man." Rather, he confidently assumed equality, appealing for support to people of all racial groups.

Moreover, this very approach of openness and willingness to work together with whites, rather than in isolation from them, or in competition with them, made it possible for Obama to embrace people of all races, and just as importantly, to be embraced by them. This is why he could speak with authority about his willingness to run for the post of President of the USA, a thought which never crossed the mind of Booker T. Washington 31 and that is why young people of all races, White and Black, Hispanic, Native American, Oriental, Caribbean.... all rejoiced at 11pm on Tuesday, November 4 2008!

Is there yet another striking parallel here between the careers of Joseph and Obama? Indeed! For, Joseph was able "to rise to the top" of the Egyptian hierarchy as a Hebrew, because he was well accepted by the Egyptians. So much so that he was given the daughter of the Egyptian priest in marriage, and so identified with the Egyptians in dress, demeanor and speech that his own blood brothers did not recognize him.(Genesis 41: 37-45; 42-44). It was only when he revealed himself that they did. He reassured them with these comforting words, at once most comforting and charged with profound theological gravitas:

"NOW THEREFORE BE NOT GRIEVED, NOR ANGRY WITH YOURSELVES, THAT YE SOLD ME HITHER: FOR GOD DID SEND ME BEFORE YOU TO PRESERVE LIFE." GENESIS 45:5

Note carefully that Joseph revealed himself to his brothers in Africa. What did Joseph mean when he spoke to his brothers in this manner? What role has Africa played in humankind's religious quest? What does all this say about the Doctrine of Divine Intervention? How is it relevant to the ascendency of Obama and the challenges we face in our own lives? These are the intriguing questions which will test and indeed tease our minds in the chapters ahead. READ ON!

CHAPTER 4

"ETHIOPIA SHALL SOON STRETCH OUT HER HANDS TO GOD"
Psalm 68:31

As we have seen in our discussion of the first clause of this verse, " The princes who shall come out of Africa," is a prophecy of the rise of Black political leaders, including such champions of racial social justice such as, MARCUS GARVEY, MARTIN LUTHER KING JR., AND OF COURSE BARACK OBAMA.

We come now to examine the second clause of this most important verse:

"Ethiopia shall soon stretch out her hands to God."

These clauses coming so closely together, must be interpreted as being related to each other. It is submitted that if the first clause foreshadows the ascendency of Blacks to political power, the second prophesies their rise to leadership in the religious and ecclesiastical aspects of humankind.

Here, it is noteworthy to reflect upon the profound influence that the "dark continent of Africa" has exerted in bringing the light of the Gospel to humankind. Indeed, at three crucial junctures in the history of the people of God, Africa figured prominently in bringing about liberation.

First, as has been discussed already, Africa served as the place of refuge for the Hebrews of antiquity. In the Joseph Narrative, it is recorded that the young Hebrew, Joseph went before the other Israelites in order to provide a place for them.

The message that Joseph sought " to get across" to his brethren was that they should not be angry for what they had done, because God had sent him ahead of them to provide a place for them to settle and graze their animals in Egypt, free from the hazards of the nomadic life.1 In accord with the Divine covenant with Abraham, God, then provided a district in Egypt (the land of Goshen), where they multiplied over a period of four hundred years, until they were rescued from bondage imposed by RAMSES II, the Pharaoh of the oppression. 2

The second time that Africa featured prominently in the Bible was at the Birth of Christ. Then, the forces of evil, personified in that most cruel of monarchs of all time, Herod the Great, sought to kill Him. But Joseph, the devout earthly Father of the Christ Child, acting in strict, uncompromising accord to the Divine Command as revealed in dreams, obediently took Mary and the Christ Child and fled with them to Egypt.3 Very significantly the Wise Men, who had gone to Herod's palace before being led to worship the Christ Child, presented Him with the gifts of gold, frankincense and myrrh. The gold gifted by the Wise Men, NO DOUBT, PROVIDED THE WHEREWITHAL FOR Joseph to escape to Egypt and remain there until after the death of Herod. As it is revealed in Holy Scripture, Joseph was divinely guided to take this action "that it might be fulfilled which was spoken of the LORD by the prophet saying,'Out of Egypt have I called my son." 4

Joseph, fully sensitive to the political events of his day, did not return to BETHLEHEM, eventually taking the Christ Child and Mary to reside in Nazareth, beyond the jurisdiction of ARCHALEUS, son of Herod. (Matt. 2:23).

What is significant to our discussion here is the fact that, according to Matthew, AFRICA served again as a place of refuge, this time for the HOLY FAMILY(Matt. 2: 13-23). For this reason, all Christians owe a debt of gratitude to Africa as the continent where Christ was protected from the machinations of those who wanted to get rid of Him. (Matt. 2:10).

The third scene is taken from the life and witness of the early Church. As the early Church began to expand as a result of the preaching of Peter at Pentecost (Acts 2) and the work of the other Apostles, evangelists and deacons, the Jewish authorities became concerned. Thereafter began the first period of the persecution of the Christians, culminating in the martyrdom of Stephen (Acts 8). As a result, several of the leaders of the Church moved beyond Jerusalem, in accord with the GREAT COMMISSION. (Matt. 28:16-20, Acts 1: 8). Prominent amongst them was the deacon Philip, who became an evangelist.5 In the course of his journeys, he met an Ethiopian. The relevant Scripture passage is most illuminating:

"And the angel of the LORD spoke unto Philip, saying, 'Arise, and go toward the south unto the way that goeth down from Jerusalem unto Gaza, which is a desert, and he arose and went: and behold, a man of Ethiopia, an eunuch of great authority under Candace queen of the Ethiopians, who had the charge of all her treasure, and had come to Jerusalem for to worship, was returning and sitting in his chariot read Esias the prophet. Then the Spirit said unto Philip, "Go near, and join thyself to this chariot. And Philip ran thither to him, and heard him read the prophet Esias, and said "Understandest thou what thou readest? And he said, 'How can I, except some man should guide me? And the place of the scripture which he read was this, "He was led as a sheep to the slaughter; and like a dumb lamb before his shearer, so he opened not his mouth. In his humiliation his judgment was taken away: and who shall declare his generation? For his life is taken from the earth. AND THE EUNUCH answered Philip and said, 'I pray thee, of whom speaketh this? Of himself, or of some other man? Then Philip opened his mouth, and began at the same scripture, and preached unto him Jesus. And as they went on their way, they came unto a certain water; and the eunuch said, "See, here is water; what doth hinder me to be baptized?" And Philip said, "If thou believest with all thine heart, thou mayest." And he answered and said, "I believe that Jesus Christ is the Son of God." And he commanded the chariot to stand still: and they went down both into the water, both Philip and the eunuch; and he baptized him. And when they were come up out of the water, the Spirit of the Lord caught away Philip, that the eunuch saw him no more: And he went on his way rejoicing. (Acts 8: 26-39AV.)

The Ethiopian official, having experienced a powerful conversion under the anointed ministry of Philip the Deacon who became an Evangelist, went on his way rejoicing. This writer has always been deeply touched by the Biblical account of this son of Africa, returning to his homeland, rejoicing after he had received Jesus the Christ as his Saviour and LORD. Could it be that this African was the first Gentile convert and one of the pioneer missionaries, who even before the great mission endeavors of Paul, carried the Gospel beyond the Holy Land?

Commenting on this seminal text, so important for an appreciation of the role of the sons and daughters of Africa in the expansion of the Church, a prominent American scholar has this to say:

"What is recorded here is of a life that was true to its light. The subject of this fragment of biography is an Ethiopian. Though a fragment, it conducts to the most critical portion of life, and puts the key of it into our hand. He is a firstfruits of the fulfillment of the prophecy that was written, 'Ethiopia shall soon stretch out her hands unto God.' (Ps. lxviii.31); and in the desolacy too rapidly drawing on Jerusalem, Zion was still to say, "This man was born in her. (Ver.28, Ps. lxxxci.5). The Ethiopian cannot "change his skin," but God can change a darkened heart, and this HE IS DOING. By what route the Divine ray of light reached the Ethiopian's mind we know not, ..." but that in man's deepest darkness that light oftentimes loves most suddenly to spring us, we do know." He was not one who had been brought up in the light of revelation, but was following that which was given him. 6

The scholar then came to the conclusion that the Ethiopian was acting in fulfillment of the prophecy of Psalm 68, that "Ethiopia would stretch forth her hands to God." Specifically, he conceives of this text as referring to the pivotal role that those coming out of Ethiopia would assume in the propagation of the word of God. The thrust of the Christian faith beyond Israel, therefore, began with this Ethiopian, who having been converted, returned to Africa to proclaim the Gospel!

That the ETHIOPIAN carried out mission work in his homeland is attested to by Blyden, who points out that "The eunuch returned to his country with his heart full of joy and peace and love – with a newborn and unquenchable enthusiasm, and became the founder, it is believed, of the Abyssinian Church, which, through various trying vicissitudes, continues to this day." 7

The Ethiopian potentate, baptized by Philip, "the first fruits of the prophecy, "Ethiopia shall stretch out her hands to God", proved to be the initiator of the long historical process, whereby the sons and daughters of the Dark Continent have contributed to bringing the light of the Gospel to humankind. Before delving further into this process, it is useful to deal with the question," What is the meaning of Ethiopia in our text?"

Well, the answer is at hand. In much of the teaching of scholars who have studied AFRICA, "Ethiopia" is used to refer to the whole of Africa. As such, this text may be applied to religious leaders who emerge from Africa to proclaim the word of God to the world. Or, to put it another way, whenever you came across this text, read "Africa" instead of "Ethiopia."

It is important to bear in mind that the continent of Africa has played a pivotal role in the expansion of Christianity. Indeed, during the period of the early Church, It was North Africa where the Christian faith was strongest. That was the part of Africa which has given us some of the greatest scholars of the faith, notably Augustine of Hippo, Clement of Alexandria, Origen and Tertullian. The Church in North Africa however, after flourishing for centuries, suffered much as a result of the advance of Islam.

The center of Christianity, then, shifted to Europe, notably Rome and has remained there up until recent times. During much of this time, Africa was known as the "Dark-Continent," not only because of the color of most of its inhabitants but also because many of its peoples were pagans. This remained so until the time of the European missionaries who went to Africa to proclaim the Gospel. Notable amongst these of course was David Livingstone (1826 - 1874), THE great missionary and explorer, who served in at least ten nations in Africa. Another leading missionary of the nineteenth century who served in Africa was Mary Slessor of Calabar, West Africa.

THE Gospel has spread rapidly through Africa ever since these missionaries of the nineteenth century labored so assiduously there. For, in addition to Livingston and Slessor, missionaries from all the major Christian nations of Europe felt the call to serve in Africa. Thus, it has been noted that:

"In 1990, the ten modern African countries where Livingstone trod the old native trails had a population of over 140 million. Of the 125 million non-white in that number, a staggering total of 75 million are Christians. There are today millions upon millions of non- white Christians in the part of Africa that got it first taste of the Gospel from David Livingstone….." 8

There can be no doubt, then, that major strides have been made during the twentieth century in the area of Leadership by the sons of Africa in the Church. For instance, the Rev. Dr. Philip Potter, a native of Dominica, a small island in Caribbean, became the President of the World Council of Churches. and served with distinction in this capacity for many years. Referred to as "the Black Pope", his elevation to a top post in the Church was symbolic of the major advances made by Christians of the third World during the mid – twentieth century. That this trend continues, is evidenced by the fact that the incumbent President of the WCC hails from Africa. 9 Yes, today we are seeing the fulfillment of that prophetic text:

"Ethiopia shall stretch out her hand to God."

Turning from ecclesiastical affairs to scholarship, it is again clear that great strides are being made by people from the Third World. Traditionally, the centers of scholarship in the Christian Church have been the countries of the North Atlantic, notably Germany, Holland, Great Britain and the United States of America. Indeed, it is not too much to assert that SCHOLARSHIP in the Christian world has been dominated by the nations of the west "from time immemorial!" This writer vividly recalls that when he embarked upon theological studies in the mid-twentieth century, very few text books he used came from the Third World.10 However, development since then has brought about a radical shift in this area. This has been manifested mainly by the emergence of the Liberationist theologies, which place priority upon social justice and identification with the oppressed. These include Liberation Theology, "being done" from the perspective of those oppressed on account of their economic status- poverty; Black Theology, "being done" from the perspective of those oppressed because of their race and Feminist Theology "being done" by those oppressed because of their gender.11 This process has been described by leading Caribbean theologians as the "decolonizing of theology "12

Major changes are taking place in the demography of the Christian world at this time, for, whereas in the nations of the North Atlantic, the traditional bastions of Christianity for the past fifteen hundred years, there is a steady decline in the number of Christians, the church is increasing "by leaps and bounds" in the countries of the third world, notably Africa, South of the Sahara, Latin American and Korea. 13 There are, therefore, tremendously important changes, impacting the development of Christianity, not only numerically, but also in terms of ecclesiastical leadership, scholarship and the focus of its mission.14 This phenomenon has been described as "The Coming of The Third Church." 15

It is expedient to examine this approach to the History of Christianity, which is conceived of in three major periods:

1. The Early Church   The Birth of Christ to Chalcedon (451)

   The First Church

2. Western Christianity   451-1950
   The Second Church

3. The Third Church   Emergence of the Liberationist theologies in the 1960s

The early Church expanded from Jerusalem into Africa, Asia and Europe, as indicated by the mission endeavors of Paul and the Ethiopian eunuch. It eventually reached Rome. The Western Church was centered at Rome for many centuries until the establishment of the Orthodox Churches and the Protestant Reformation. The Third Church, in contrast to the Western Church, consists mainly of peoples from the nations of the Third World. The epicenter of Christianity, numerically speaking at least, is gradually moving from the North (the nations of the North Atlantic) to the South (the nations of the Third World, including "Africa south of the Sahara").16 This is precisely why it is expected that soon and very soon, many more missionaries will come out of Africa and Asia to preach the Gospel to many who have not heard it, or for whom the Gospel has lost its appeal, in the developed nations of the North. Concisely, mission activity will become "more and more" a two way street in which missionaries will go from the Third World to preach the Gospel to people in the DEVELOPED nations, even as missionaries continue to come from those nations to the Third World, instead of the traditional "one way street mission activities of the past, when missionaries from the developed Western nations went out to preach the gospel to the lost souls in the pagan countries of the "dark Continent" and other Countries of the Third World! 17 Thus, an English missionary, on being welcomed to serve in Jamaica, pointed out that there were many more persons in London, his home, than there were in Jamaica, who had not responded to the Gospel.

Already, then, this process of "two way street missions" is in operation in virtually all major denominations of Christianity. The writer, for instance, knows several colleagues, who received their theological education in the Caribbean, and are now serving in congregations, mission boards and seminaries in Great Britain, Canada and the USA. As has been pointed out, churchmen from the Third World have for a long time occupied positions of authority in the World Council of Churches. In the ROMAN CATHOLIC CHURCH, there are a growing number of clergy from the developing nations, occupying top posts, including Bishops, Archbishops and Cardinals, in it's hierarchy. Moreover, there are organizations such as the International Fellowship of Third World Scholars and the rapidly expanding and influential International Conference of Third World Leaders, led by dynamic evangelist, motivator and writer, Myles Munroe, which is dedicated to improving the scholarship contributions and leadership skills of clergy and lay persons from throughout the world. All these exciting developments certainly vindicate the prophecy:

"ETHIOPIA SHALL SOON STRETCH OUT HER HANDS TO GOD!"

If, by now you are wondering "what in the world does all this have to do with Barack Obama? " That is quite understandable! Nevertheless, it is submitted that the ascendency of Barack Obama to the world's most powerful political office has profound religious ramifications as well as the obvious political implications.

Bear with me therefore, as I seek to pour into your spirit my testimony of how this event has impacted my own spiritual endeavor.

As a child growing up in a Christian Family, attending Church and Sunday School, I was indeed, deeply touched by the wonderful story of Joseph – his dreams, the gift of the "coat of many colors" from his doting Father, and the jealousy of his brothers who sold him to traders on their way to Egypt. In my youthful years, I admired the manner in which he was promoted to the top administrative post, despite adversities, including the treachery of Pharaoh's sex-starved wife and a term in prison. This display of ability certainly appealed to me at the time in my life when I, like most young people was looking for a role model of male leadership.18

Then, as I engaged in critical study of the Biblical texts at tertiary level, doubts invaded my mind with regard to the meteoric rise to power of a Hebrew young man at a time when they were regarded with disdain by the Egyptians (Gen. Ch. 41). Such rapid promotion of one belonging to the lower echelons of society to such prominence seemed all the more unlikely as I engaged in a study of the oppression of the Hebrews by the Pharaohs of a later dynasty.

As we have already seen, the promotion of a Hebrew to the post of viceroy of PHARAOH WOULD HAVE BEEN NOTHING LESS THAN "breaking news" in Ancient Egypt. One need only examine the text to realize how revolutionary was the act of Pharaoh in delegating so much authority to a young Hebrew wiseman.19

"And PHARAOH SAID UNTO Joseph, 'see, I have set thee over all the land of Egypt. And Pharaoh took off his ring from his hand, and put it upon Joseph's hand, and arrayed him in vestures of fine linen, and put a gold chain about his neck; and he made him to ride in the second chariot which he had: and they cried before, "Bow the knee: and he made him a ruler over all the land of Egypt. And Joseph was thirty years old when he stood before Pharaoh king of Egypt, And Joseph went out from the presence of Pharaoh, and went throughout all the land of Egypt." Genesis 41: 41-43, 46.

Now, in order to appreciate the tremendous amount of authority that Pharaoh delegated to Joseph, it is essential to rid our minds completely of any idea of democracy as we know it today. The Pharaohs of ancient Egypt wielded complete political power. There was no parliament or any legislative body elected by the people to limit the monarch's authority. According to our text, Pharaoh voluntarily surrendered much of his authority to the young Hebrew. The handing over of the Pharaoh's signet ring, dressing Joseph in fine linen and his wearing of a gold chain all were symbolic of the delegation of total administrative authority to this remarkable young man. As such, he became Pharaoh's viceroy, able to act with the full gravity of complete support from Pharaoh.20 who only kept ceremonial power, leaving Joseph to govern his vast domain.

Thus, according to the Biblical accounts, whereas Pharaoh, the Egyptian monarch reigned, it was Joseph, the Hebrew "upstart", who actually ruled in ancient Egypt!!!!!!

As I reflected critically upon this arrangement, my skepticism with regard to the authenticity of the "Joseph Narrative" increased. For, it seemed to me almost incredible that a Hebrew, a member of a despised lower class from a nomadic tribe, could ascend to the highest post in Ancient Egypt. It appeared to be inconceivable that the proud Egyptians would allow such a thing to happen. Indeed, I HAD REACHED THE POINT OF REGARDING THE "JOSEPH NARRATIVE as little more than fiction, some sort of Biblical fairy tale!

Then Barack Obama burst upon the scene in an amazing rally in which he announced his intention to seek the nomination of the Democratic Party for the Presidency of the USA. And just twenty months afterwards, he emerged as the first African – American President Elect in the history of the United States of America.

Reflecting upon the amazing success of Obama, with its rallying cry of "change and "job creation" AT A TIME WHEN THE WORLD WAS ENTERING INTO A RECESSION I could not help "going back to the Bible" and thinking about how Joseph was promoted to the post of Viceroy of Pharaoh moving through the ranks at a very rapid pace!

I said to myself, "Well, if Obama has been able to move from relative obscurity to become President Elect of the USA in such a short time, today, then it must have been possible for Joseph, a worshipper of the One True God, to have done so in Ancient Egypt." 21

Thus, in a sense most profound, the rapid ascendancy of Obama in the political arena, strengthened and encouraged me in my own scholastic and spiritual journey of faith.HALLELUJAH!

CHAPTER 5
"THE DIVINE ARCHITECT"

"Now therefore be not grieved, nor angry with yourselves, that ye sold me hither: for God did send me before you to preserve life."

Genesis 45:5

"And we know that in all things God works for the good of those who love Him, who have been called according to His purpose."

Romans 8:28, NIV.

"DOES GOD GUIDE ME?" "DOES GOD HAVE A PLAN FOR MY LIFE?" IF SO, HOW CAN I KNOW THIS PLAN?" IF GOD DOES HAVE A PLAN OR PURPOSE FOR MY LIFE, THEN DOES THIS NOT MEAN THAT I HAVE NO FREEDOM, THAT I MUST CONFORM TO IT OR GO TO HELL?"

While questions such as these have been asked by "people in all walks of life" from time immemorial, they emerge as especially poignant in the context of the acute socio-economic, political, moral and spiritual challenges we inevitably encounter in the world today. As a matter of fact, they have much in common, in that in the final analysis, they have to do with what has been described as "the supreme relationship" – the manner in which Almighty God, and mortal humankind relate to each other in the vicissitudes of life. Concisely, the burden of these questions may be stated thus: "How do you square the doctrine of divine sovereignty (that God is Omnipotent–all powerful, Omniscient – all knowing, and Omnipresent – present everywhere") with the principle of human freedom/responsibility?

Throughout the ages, priests, prophets, philosophers and lay people "in all walks of life: have grappled with these questions. And it may be truly said that they have "come up" with answers which have proved to be many and varied. While it is beyond the ambit of this present study to enter into detailed discussions of all these complex deliberations, it is worthwhile to carry out a survey of the three main categories into which they may be divided, with a view to demonstrating their relevance to our concern here – Obama in Prophecy!

THE DIVINE WATCHMAN

The relationship between Divine Sovereignty and human freedom or responsibility has proved to be "the bone of contention" between Christian theologians from the days of the Early Church (or "The first Church") until the present!

It was, indeed, the subject of sharp theological controversy between Augustine of Hippo, who insisted on the sovereignty of God, and Pelagius, who championed the cause of human freedom. There was no resolution, and it can be asserted with confidence, that this debate has continued ever since.1 Indeed, the classic debates of these two eminent theologians of the Early Church have set the pattern for discussions of same throughout the ages. What, then can we say of them?

First, there have been and continue to be those theologians and "schools of thought," which following in the footsteps of Augustine, have placed high priority upon Divine Sovereignty. Emphasizing the attributes of God, they have tended to highlight the distance between The Holy God and sinful humankind. Those who hold to this doctrine have found Biblical warrant, especially in the Old Testament account of the Creation (Gen. 1-2), the teaching of the Prophets (Isaiah, 40:12 -19; Amos 5:8-9), The Psalms and the book of Job.(Job 38-39) In the New Testament they have found support for teaching the all encompassing sovereignty of God. (eg. 1 John 17 and Colossians 1:15-17). The positive aspect herein, is that God is the Protector of all who trust in Him. This is the encouraging message of Psalm 121.The problematic side however, is the tendency to reduce to a minimum the freedom and responsibility of the individual, who like Job may feel overwhelmed by the Divine sovereignty and thus unable to exercise his/her responsibility. (Job 42:1-6).

Children, especially those who are brought up under such a theological approach, may feel threatened because God is always watching them. It is not too much then, to suggest that from this perspective, God is perceived as "The Great WATCHMAN," who meticulously examines and watches over every detail of our lives, leaving little or no place for our participation, freedom and responsibility.

THE DIVINE WATCHMAKER

Then, there are those thinkers, who siding with Pelagius, have placed the priority upon human responsibility to such an extent that they have tended to place GOD at the periphery, rather than at the center of the universe.

A major school of thought belonging to this category, which was quite influential in the eighteenth Century is known as "DEISM".2 THE ADVOCATES of Deism held that God, at the beginning of creation, set the world in action and then left humankind to do "pretty well" AS IT LIKED. They did not believe that God intervened in the course of history, but was aloof and far removed from the activities of humankind. Also belonging to this category are the various forms of Humanism and that particularly challenging contemporary manner of thinking – "The New Atheism." 3

It is submitted therefore, that if those schools of thought in theology which place priority upon divine sovereignty, without attributing due authority to the concept of human freedom/responsibility conceive of God as "The Divine Watchman", then those at the opposite extreme which emphasize human responsibility, without acknowledging Divine transcendence, may be regarded as conceiving of Him as "THE DIVINE WATCHMAKER." With regard to the latter, it has to be observed that there are many in the world today, who while not articulating adherence to the same, live in such a way day by day – carrying out their mundane tasks and commitments without acknowledging or realizing the authority of God – that it is painfully evident that they have implicitly embraced its values, principles, and indeed weltanchung!

THE DIVINE ARCHITECT – EXPOSITION OF THE DOCTRINE OF DIVINE INTERVENTION

On the basis of our discussion thus far, we can assert that neither of the opposing positions mentioned provide a satisfactory answer to the question. "How do you square the doctrine of Divine Sovereignty with the principle of human freedom?"

Whereas that approach which conceives of God as "The Divine Watchman" does not do justice to the concept of human responsibility, that which conceives of Him as "The Divine Watchmaker" tends to place far too much confidence in human ability, without a corresponding demonstration of faith in God.

All this begs the question, "is there then, an approach to the matter under discussion here, which while attributing due recognition to Divine Sovereignty, does not compromise the principle of human freedom /responsibility?" The answer is at hand, being in the affirmative. It may be described as "The Doctrine of Divine Intervention." In contrast to Deism, which leaves little or no place for God to intervene in human affairs, it teaches that God, in His infinite wisdom and deep concern for the welfare of humankind, does indeed intervene in the events of time and history. On the other hand, in contrast to those concepts which place priority upon Divine control to such an extent so as to obliterate human freedom, this doctrine calls for the full exercise of human responsibility. As such, it is submitted that it provides the basis and rationale for the most plausible explanation for the emergence of Barack Obama, from a Biblical perspective.

It is important therefore, to further expound this doctrine as we continue to discuss the profound Biblical and theological ramifications of the rise of Barack Obama from relative obscurity just a few years ago, to become one of the most influential and recognizable persons on planet Earth at this crucial juncture in humankind's religious and theological quest!

So as we have seen, the doctrine which places priority upon Divine sovereignty is based on the concept of God as "The Divine Watchman," and its counterpart at the other extreme, which places the emphasis on human freedom may be described as being based upon the concept of God as "The Divine Watchmaker." It is suggested that envisioning God as "The Divine Architect" is most illuminating in explaining the doctrine of Divine Intervention.

In this regard, let us bear in mind that the Bible has much to say about building things. Thus, warned by God to prepare for the flood, Noah built the Ark. (Genesis 6: 11-22). God gave elaborate instructions to Moses with regard to the erection of the Tabernacle in the wilderness (Exodus 25-30.) Moreover, Solomon was inspired by God in the building of the Temple. (II Chron. 2) Whereas Ezra, as we have seen, was instrumental in the rebuilding of the Temple, Nehemiah took the initiative in rebuilding the walls of Jerusalem after the exile. (Neh. 1-4)

Paul, a tent maker, spoke of the Church as being built on a firm foundation. The writer of the book of Hebrews vividly described Abraham as having a vision of a city whose Builder and Architect was God. (Heb. 11:10.) Jesus of Nazareth was a carpenter, and according to tradition, a very skilled one.

There is therefore, solid Biblical warrant for drawing an analogy from the field of human endeavour known as "building," to describe the nature and activity of God, The Divine Architect.

I vividly recall that several years ago, my wife and I had a desire to build our own home. Having resided in manses provided by the church for many years, we realized that the time had come for us to build a residence that we and our children could call our own home.

So we consulted with an architect. In doing so, it was our impression that he would draw a plan, we would pay him for same and then get a building contractor to construct it. However, he explained that he would help us in the design of our home (based on the vision for it.), draw the plans, and then he would personally visit the site during construction to see how the workmen were getting along with it. They were expected to build it in accordance with the plan the architect had drawn. If they made mistakes, or failed to follow the plan, then he assured us that it was his responsibility "to get them back on track." The architect then, had a vision of how the building would look when completed, had drawn a plan to guide the workmen, and made a commitment to continue to supervise the building of the house until it was completed in a satisfactory manner, so that we could make it "home." 4

Bearing the role of the architect in mind, it is possible to understand the concept of God as The Divine Architect, in the context of the Doctrine of Divine Intervention.

Proceeding further, it is submitted that seven seminal principles inform the Doctrine of Divine Intervention. Here they are!

1. GOD, THE DIVINE ARCHITECT HAS A PLAN/DESIGN FOR THE WORLD. AT THE HEART OF THE Doctrine of Divine Intervention is the conviction that God, The Creator, has a plan for His creation.5 This is solidly based on the Biblical doctrine of Creation in Genesis 1-2. He, then may be described as The Divine Architect, who created the world for a purpose. As the Psalmist put it, "The earth is the Lord's and the fullness thereof, the world and all they that dwell therein. (Psalm 24:1).

2. THE DIVINE ARCHITECT HAS A PLAN AND PURPOSE FOR THE LIFE OF EVERY HUMAN BEING.6 This leads directly to the second principle. Not only does the Divine Architect have a purpose for the world; he has a purpose and plan for the life of every human being. We have not been placed here on planet Earth by chance. Rather, God having created us and endowed us with gifts, expects us to use them to the best of our respective abilities.

3. GOD DOES INTERVENE IN HISTORY AND THE EVENTS OF THE LIFE OF THE INDI-

VIDUAL IN ACCORD WITH HIS PURPOSE.
4. YOU SHOULD GIVE YOURSELF ASSIDOUSLY TO DISCOVERING THE DIVINE ARCHITECT'S PURPOSE (VISION) FOR YOUR LIFE.
5. WHEN YOU ACT IN THIS MANNER YOU ARE ON THE WAY TO FULFILLING GOD'S PURPOSE FOR YOUR LIFE.
6. NEVERTHELESS, YOU CAN THWART (BLOCK) GOD'S PURPOSE FOR YOUR LIFE BY BEING "DISOBEDIENT TO THE VISION"
7. BUT "THE GOOD NEWS IS THAT YOU CAN" "GET BACK ON TRACK" BY BEING PENITENT. AT THE HEART OF THE GOSPEL IS GOD'S RESTORATION OF THE SINNER.

THEREFORE YOU REALIZE YOUR TRUE POTENTIAL AND FULFILL THE PURPOSE OF YOUR EXISTENCE BY LIVING DAY BY DAY IN HARMONY WITH THE PLAN OF THE DIVINE ARCHITECT FOR YOUR LIFE.

This Doctrine of Divine Intervention is both observable and reassuring. For instance, the late Rev. Dr. Hugh Sherlock, prominent Caribbean Churchman, applied it to the history of the Church in terms of "three divine interventions." 7 Its principles certainly can be discerned in examining the life of Joseph, which as we have already seen, has striking parallels to that of Barack Obama.

We assert confidently therefore, that God has a plan for His world. In order to appreciate the significance of "the Joseph Narrative," it has to be placed in the context of the Divine plan for the redemption of the People of God. In the Abrahamic covenant, God promised to protect his descendants, through whom all the families of the earth would be blessed.(Gen. 12:1-3)

The Divine intention to protect the People of God is proclaimed in the Hexateuch, the first six books of the Bible. As von Rad points out:

"THE BASIC THEME OF THE HEXATEUCH MAY BE STATED AS FOLLOWS: GOD, THE CREATOR OF THE WORLD CALLED THE PATRIARCHS AND PROMISED THEM THE LAND OF CANAAN. WHEN ISRAEL BECAME NUMEROUS IN EGYPT, GOD LED THE PEOPLE THROUGH THE WILDERNESS WITH WONDERFUL DEMONSTRATIONS OF GRACE, THEN AFTER THEIR LENGTHY WANDERING HE GAVE THEM UNDER JOSHUA THE PROMISED LAND." (Von Rad, p. 14.).8

We come to understand the significance of the Joseph Narrative when we ask the question," Why did the Israelites have to sojourn in the land of Egypt? How did it fit in with the Divine plan for the preservation of the people of God?"

Let us then continue our study of the Joseph Narrative, bearing in mind the Doctrine of Divine Intervention. For, from this perspective, it is revealing, fascinating and relevant to our basic concern here – Obama in prophecy.

The referenced Doctrine of Divine Intervention permeates the Joseph Narrative "from start to finish." We already have discussed the broad span of Joseph's life. However, it is of interest to highlight three specific aspects to demonstrate that his life's path was determined by the divine purposes, superintended by God.

Firstly let's look at the dreams of Joseph as a boy, which generally speaking, have been taken in a negative light. Joseph is portrayed as a young "spoiled brat" whose lofty dreams and gift of a coat of many colours from his father incurs the wrath of his jealous brothers, who eventually sell him into slavery. However, viewed from the perspective of all that eventually transpired, when they surely did bow down to him as the ruler of Egypt, the dreams may be understood as the means through which God had conveyed to Joseph His purpose for his life. KIDNER'S comment here is most revelatory:

"The account of the dreams, coming at the outset makes God, not Joseph, the 'hero' of the story; it is not a tale of human success but of divine sovereignty."[9]

Secondly, there is the incident of Potiphar's wife, whose treachery resulted in the imprisonment of Joseph. It has to be pointed out here, that while it was an evil act on her part, it led eventually to the promotion of Joseph to the top post, For, while in prison, he met Pharaoh's butler, who told the Egyptian king about him as being an expert interpreter of dreams. Joseph's punishment was not a severe as it might have been. Though wrongly accused, such convictions often exacted the death penalty. He was thrown into prison because "the unfolding story makes it obvious that God who had brought him there, was preserving him for his task." GOD'S purpose was being fulfilled despite the machinations of men and women![10]

Thirdly, there is the scene in which Joseph reveals himself to his brethren in Egypt. After a period of putting them to the test, having sent them back home to get their younger brother, he reveals himself to them as their long-lost brother. It is interesting to note that all along there were those amongst his brothers, notably Reuben and Judah, who expressed the opinion that they were being punished by God for the manner in which they had treated their little brother! This expression of the doctrine of divine reward and retribution, is in keeping with the contention that the Joseph Narrative is Wisdom Literature. It is then that Joseph reveals himself to his fearful brethren with these immortal words:

> "Now, therefore be not grieved, nor angry with yourselves, that you sold me hither: for God did send me before you to preserve life."

This verse is the key to understanding the Joseph Narrative, which occupies nearly a third of the book of Genesis. Essentially, it teaches that all the events of the life of Joseph were directed by God as a means of preserving His people. Yes to recapitulate, the dreams of the boy Joseph, his coat of many colours, which caused his jealous brothers to sell him into slavery in Egypt, the cunning of Potophar's wife leading to his imprisonment, his interpretation of dreams leading to his introduction to Pharaoh and eventual promotion to the post of Pharaoh's viceroy (CEO of Egypt) all were part and parcel of the divine plan for the life of Joseph!

We see then that, "the ups and downs" manifested in the eventful experiences of Joseph were all directed towards the preservation of the People of God at a crucial juncture in their historical development.

More than four hundred years after the palmy days of Joseph as Pharaoh's viceroy in Egypt, when the Israelites were settled in the Promised Land, they realized that it was within the mysterious workings of Divine Providence, "The Right Hand of God", that their ancestors had to sojourn in that most ancient African land. Thus, at harvest time, the farmer, having experienced prosperity in a land "flowing with milk and honey", presented a basket of fruit to God, expressing gratitude for Divine Blessings by repeating the creed:

"A Syrian ready to perish was my father, and he went

down into Egypt, and sojourned there with a few, and became there a nation, great, mighty and populous:

And the Egyptians evil treated us, and afflicted us and laid upon us hard bondage:

And when we cried unto the LORD GOD of our fathers, the Lord heard our voice, and looked on our affliction, and our labour, and our oppression:

And the Lord brought us forth out of Egypt with a mighty hand, and with an outstretched arm, and great terribleness, and with signs and wonders: And He hath brought us into this place, and hath given us this land, even a land that floweth with milk and honey."

Deut. 26: 5-9

Thus the reason why Joseph had to go down into Egypt moves into sharp perspective, becoming abundantly clear! As already noted, God had entered ito a covenant with Abraham, the founding Patriarch, promising to multiply his progeny beyond reckoning, to protect them and to lead them into the Promised Land.

Jacob and his family surely were in dire straits when he sent his sons to Egypt to buy grain for themselves and their cattle. It was not just a matter of JACOB being an "Aramean ready to perish;" rather it was a matter of "life and death" for him and all who remained with him in Canaan. BEAR IN mind that they were nomads, depending upon their livestock for survival. There was a very severe famine in that land. Indeed judging from reports of the suffering in times of famine in antiquity, or under siege with their enemies depriving them of food, nomads resorted to eating all their precious livestock and even to acts of cannibalism.11 This is why old Jacob acidly admonished his sons " Why don't you do something? I hear that there is grain in Egypt, go there and buy some to keep us from starving to death." Yes, starving to death," that was the grim reality which threatened the very existence of those nomads, had they remained in Canaan!

Joseph by sovereign design was sent to Egypt ahead of the rest of his family, and was promoted to a top post, so that he would be in a position to provide a safe place for them in Egypt, which in contrast to their hungry homeland, was a land of great bounty. Indeed, Joseph was able to arrange for them to live in Goshen, where they could carry out their shepherding and increase their numbers as proclaimed by God in the Abrahamic covenant.

It is as we reflect on these things that we realize that in the Joseph Narrative, there is a wonderful demonstration of the workings of Divine Providence. It is certainly an example par excellence of the Doctrine of Divine Intervention. All the events of the Life of Joseph, including the dreams, the jealousy of his brothers, the deception of Potiphar's wife, his imprisonment, revelation of the dreams of Pharaoh and his meteoric rise to power are seen as part and parcel of the redemptive work of God. Thus we concur, the real hero in the "Joseph Narrative" is not Joseph but the Lord! The message here is that God indeed works in and through events to bring about his purposes. Indeed, whether he is conceived of in terms of the Aristotlean First Cause, or the Grand WEAVER, or as suggested here, "The Divine Architect," the essential message about Him is the same – God is willing and able to work out the salvation of those who are obedient to His vision for them. This is all well summed up by St. Paul in these immortal words to the Christians, in danger of suffering at Rome:

"AND WE KNOW THAT IN ALL THINGS GOD WORKS FOR THE GOOD OF THOSE WHO LOVE HIM, WHO HAVE BEEN CALLED ACCORDING TO HIS PURPOSE." (Romans 8:28, NIV.)12

HALLELUJAH!!!!!!!!!!!!!

CHAPTER 6
"YES, WE CAN!"

There was a time when, there flourished in certain religious circles in the United States of America, a theological school known as "Dispensationalism."1 Its advocates conceived of the activities of God in terms of specific periods of time, "or ages" or "dispensations," during which they were done once and not repeated. For instance, they held tenaciously to the teaching that the performance of miracles belonged to Biblical times and as such there was no need to look for miracles in the modern age or "dispensation."

In stark contrast to this approach, which limits the activity of God in a particular manner to a definite age, the Doctrine of Divine Intervention holds that the action of God is not to be contained in any particular age, as He can intervene at any stage in the history of nations or the life of persons, to bring about changes in accord with His purpose for them.

We have demonstrated its principles as operative in the life of Joseph. It is therefore, appropriate to apply same to that of Obama. In this regard, it is sufficient to point out that we have already noted a number of striking parallels between the Biblical account of the Patriarch, who arose from servitude, to prominence in Egypt and that of the contemporary, charismatic African - American who has emerged from boyhood in Hawaii, to the summit of political authority in Washington. It is therefore not necessary to reiterate them here. There are however, others which merit consideration!

For instance, as we have demonstrated, Joseph, from childhood in Canaan, was endowed with a sense of a special purpose for his life, foreshadowed by his dreams. Thus, the events of his early life in Canaan, and as a young man in Egypt, all were designed to groom him for leadership in Egypt, to position him so that he could help his brethren in a time of great need.

Likewise, in reading the account of the formative years of Obama in Hawaii, one cannot escape feeling, that here was a young man who was being prepared for leadership. Obama admits that the members of the family, in which he grew up were not deeply religious! Despite this so - called secular environment however, it was evident that his Mother undoubtedly believed that her son was destined for greatness. During those formative years, his Mother would wake him up at 4 am., so that she could provide tutoring for him, in addition to his attendance at day school. Special emphasis was placed on English. Yes, every morning religiously, she made him get up to read to her; to read properly, write and read again and again. Whenever the child complained, she explained that it was for his benefit, not hers, that she made the sacrificial effort to teach him English every morning. It is most salutary to bear in mind that the excellent skills in oral and verbal communications demonstrated by the African - American in his rallying cry, "YES, WE CAN" which proved so effective in highly motivational and inspiring speeches on the campaign trail and in the all important Presidential debates, has its genesis in these childhood lessons given him by his mother![2]

Moreover, as we have seen, Joseph possessed a keen mind, alert so that he could move ahead "at the most opportune moment." Thus, when he had wisely urged the powerful Egyptian monarch to establish a grain feeding program in view of the impending famine, he made it clear that he would be willing to organize it. As a result, he was in a position in Egypt to provide a place of refuge for his brethren in a time of severe drought.

Likewise, Obama has proved to be gifted with the ability to see opportunities coming his way and to grasp them. As a master orator, he was also able to capture the imaginations and win the hearts of those who came to hear him. He certainly inspired confidence when he spoke. Just as Joseph's interpretation of PHAROAH'S dreams launched his rapid rise power, so it was the speech that Obama made at the Democratic Convention in 2004, which catapulted him into national prominence.3 Obama, like Joseph being a 'bridge' personality, could bring people of different racial backgrounds together. That is why his speech at the Democratic convention proved so appealing: "There is not a White America or a Black America.. There is the United States of America."

Moreover, during his campaign, Obama inspired those who came to hear him with the rallying cry, "YES, WE CAN!" "People in all walks of life," representing all races, religions and nationalities, responded to this appeal and so were inspired to believe that they too could accomplish great things.

Turning back to Joseph, it is essential to note that he was willing to act in accord with God's purpose for his life. Thus, in his position as Pharaoh's viceroy, he took measures to bring about a great degree of economic prosperity for the Egyptian nation. More significantly, however, he provided a place in Egypt for his family. He certainly was in a position 'to get even with them' for how they had treated him. But realizing in that it was in accord with the Divine Plan for the saving of his people, he treated them with great charity, after an initial period of testing them!

Again, it is most interesting to note that Obama, from

childhood and certainly during his years as a young adult, had a sense of being called to fulfill a purpose. This is why, having graduated from Harvard Law School, he did not take up a post in a prestigious law company, which could have provided a big salary and security for life. Instead, he decided to work in Chicago as a community organizer, a post which required much dedication with very little monetary gain. Whether he saw it in that light, I do not know. However, this writer cannot help believing that in electing to serve as a community worker, Obama was acting in concert with the plan of the Divine Architect for his life.

It is now most appropriate that we pause to carry out a candid evaluation of the life of Obama, from a religious and theological perspective. Here, opinions most widely divergent have been expressed by both clergy and laypersons. There have been those, on the one hand who have vested him with nearly messianic status. At the other extreme are those who have gone so far as to suggest that he is "the anti-Christ," despite the fact that there is no Biblical warrant for such an outlandish claim, or better a caricature! And although he has made it clear that he is a Christian, there are those, who insist that he is Muslim, one reason being "bandied about" is that it is evident in his Christian names – Barack Hussein!

IT IS SUBMITTED, HOWEVER, ON THE BASIS OF OUR STUDY, THAT NONE OF THESE CLAIMS DOES JUSTICE TO THE FAITH OF OBAMA. THIS WRITER MAINTAINS THAT THE BEST WAY TO EXPLAIN THE EMERGENCE OF BARACK (WHICH MEANS "BLESSED" BOTH IN HEBREW AND ARABIC!) OBAMA, FROM A BIBLICAL PERSPECTIVE, IS IN TERMS OF THE DOCTRINE OF DIVINE INTERVENTION – THAT GOD, IN HIS INFINITE WISDOM, HAS INTERVENED IN HUMAN HISTORY TO BRING ABOUT THE ELECTION OF OBAMA AS PRESIDENT OF THE UNITED STATES OF AMERICA AT THIS

CRUCIAL WATERSHED IN THE HISTORICAL DEVELOPMENT OF HUMANKIND.

AS A SCHOLAR OF THE OLD TESTAMENT, I BELIEVE THAT JOSEPH WAS RAISED UP BY GOD IN ANTIQUITY TO PROVIDE A SAFE PLACE OF REFUGE FOR THE CHILDREN OF ISRAEL AT A TIME OF SEVERE FAMINE WHICH THREATENED THEIR VERY EXISTENCE. AS A METHODIST, I HAVE ALWAYS BELIEVED THAT GOD RAISED UP JOHN AND CHARLES WESLEY TO PROCLAIM THE GOSPEL IN ENGLAND DURING THE EIGHTEENTH CENTURY AT A TIME OF SPIRITUAL CRISIS.

CONCISELY, LIKE JOSEPH OF ANTIQUITY, AND THE WESLEY BROTHERS OF THE EIGHTEENTH CENTURY IN ENGLAND, GOD HAS RAISED UP BARACK OBAMA TO FULFILL A PARTICULAR CALLING AT THIS TIME.

THIS IS BUT AN ACT OF THE SOVEREIGN GOD WHO HAS CREATED THE EARTH AND WHO INTERVENES IN THE AFFAIRS OF HUMANKIND, IN ACCORD WITH HIS PLAN FOR IT.

Now, as we have seen, two of the principles of this doctrine are that God has a plan for the whole world, and that He does intervene in human events in accord with His will. There is also the principle that God has a purpose for the life of every person.

That God has a purpose for the life of each and every human being upon planet Earth, as already indicated, is one of the cardinal principles of the Doctrine of Divine Intervention. This must be a message which the Lord is strongly impressing upon His people "in the world today." For theologians as diverse as Norman Vincent Peale 4 and Cardinal Sheen 5 of the mid twentieth century as well as contemporary contributions including from Dr. Myles Munroe,6

Bishop T.D. Jakes,7 Joyce Meyers,8 Bishop Neil Ellis,9 Dr. Rodney Smothers,10 Dr. Yvonne Capehart,11 and of course Joel Osteen12 and Rick Warren13 concur in placing priority upon the concept of purpose in the life of the believer, "in the world today." All this is in keeping with the teaching of the late PROFESSOR PAUL Tillich, that the major phobia of humankind is the fear of the meaninglessness! 14

READER, THIS MEANS THAT GOD HAS A PLAN for your life….. and mine!

But it does not end there. According to the third AND OTHER PRINCIPLES, THE DIVINE ARCHITECT WANTS YOU TO DISCOVER THAT PURPOSE AND TO GIVE YOURSELF ASSIDUOUSLY TO FULLFILLING IT. ONLY IN THIS WAY WILL YOU BE ENABLED TO WALK IN VICTORY.

This does seem like a tall order. Most challenging!

INDEED, WE MAY ASK OURSELVES, "CAN WE KNOW THE PURPOSES THAT THE DIVINE ARCHITECT HAS DETERMINED FOR OUR LIVES AND FULFILL THEM EVEN IF WE FACE CHALLENGES ALONG THE WAY?"

THE ANSWER IS NOW A FAMILIAR ONE:

"YES WE CAN!"

HOW?

ADELANTE!

READ ON!

CHAPTER 7
"GO IN THE DIRECTION OF YOUR DREAMS"

> "And it shall come to pass afterward, that I will pour out my Spirit upon all flesh; and your sons and your daughters shall prophesy, your old men shall dream dreams, your young men shall see visions:"
>
> Joel 2:28

Throughout this study, we have been engaged in an exciting and most illuminating comparison between the lives of the ancient Patriarch Joseph and the contemporary politician Barack Obama. And while we have been impressed by the striking parallels between them, we also have noted that there are significant differences.

For, both arose from the ranks of minority groups to positions of top leadership, the former in ancient Egypt, and the latter in the present day USA. However, whereas Joseph was arbitrarily promoted to a top post by a benevolent despot, the Pharaoh, who knew nothing about "government by the people," Obama was elected to leadership by the people exercising their democratic right to vote.

There can be no doubt however, as our study has demonstrated, that both Joseph and Obama rose rapidly to leadership because they were men of vision, with a strong sense purpose, endowed with the alertness to recognize the opportunities for advancement which came their way, and the courage to employ to the fullest, their God-given talents to grasp them!

What, then, is the main lesson that we can learn from the examples of these two leaders, to assist us in our own endeavours as we seek to cope with the challenges and opportunities we may encounter in our trek through this transitory time on Earth? It is submitted, that in the light of our reflection thus far, the answer is at our disposal!

Surely, it is none other than that in this process, we need a vision to guide and inspire us, faith and the courage and perseverance to turn it into reality.

Whence then comes this vision? That is the next question which comes to mind. Well, as has been pointed out, a cardinal principle of the Doctrine of Divine Intervention, is that God, The Divine Architect, has a plan and a purpose for your life. Thus, the vision, the dream which inspires and guides us comes from the Lord. It is essentially speaking, the imprint in our minds of the plan that God has for our life. As has been demonstrated in the case of Joseph, for instance, his childhood dreams were the means whereby the purpose of God for his life was revealed to him. It was only after he recognized his brothers in Egypt, many years later, that he realized that such was indeed the case. This is precisely why it is so important that you should discover what is God's plan for your life. For, as the Rev. Dr. Nymphas Edwards emphasized, the vision you have is from the LORD.1

It is of benefit to pause here to ponder more carefully this whole matter of God providing us a vision, and our responsibility to work towards fulfilling it. Not only does the Divine Architect have a plan for our life., He also equips us with gifts, talents and abilities to realize our dreams, to fulfill the purposes He has in store for us.

This is surely, the lesson of the Parable of the Talents given for our guidance by the Master (Matt. 25:14-30). Note that while one person gets five talents, another two and the third just one, there is no servant who gets none! Sometimes, we hear people, in moods of dejection and self – pity complaining that they have no talent. Nothing can be farther from the truth! It is clear that God, the Great Architect provides every person with at least one talent. Yes, there are those gifted "super heroes," people who may have many talents. And there are the vast majority who get by on a few talents. But there is not a single individual on planet Earth who has no talent at all. Note well then, that the person who had the one talent was not condemned because he had just one. RATHER IT was precisely because he did not use that which he had, and so forfeited it to the wealthy man (the billionaire so to speak) who already had more than anyone else.

The lesson of this parable is certainly in keeping with the fourth of the principles of the Doctrine of Divine Intervention – It is our responsibility, having discerned God's purpose for our life to give ourselves diligently to achieving it! 2

The importance of discerning the plan of the Divine Architect for your life as early as possible, can hardly be over emphasized. I can testify that from as long as I can remember, it has been my desire to serve as a Minister of the Gospel. Indeed, my mother (of blessed memory) often told her colleagues that from early childhood, I would erect a makeshift pulpit and preach to a congregation composed of children in our neighborhood. Thus, it was with great delight that I was ordained to the ministry by the late Rev. Dr. Hugh Sherlock who, as has been pointed out, was a staunch advocate of the Doctrine of Divine Intervention. So, from early childhood I knew the Lord's vision for my life. By contrast, my brother did not finally decide upon the profession to which he devoted his life until he had completed his secondary education.

Recently, a minister preaching at the 40th Anniversary of a church, noted that whereas forty years was a short time in the life of an institution, it is a very long time in the life of a person.3 He asserted that by age forty a person should long before then, have decided upon the goal for his / her life. He went on to point out that regretfully, there are persons who reach that age who are still not sure what they want to do with lives. Indeed, it has been the observation of this writer that persons who reach that age without knowing their purpose seldom achieve much!

Give yourself, then, assiduously, diligently and relentlessly, not only to the understanding of the Divine Architect's plan for your life; but also to fulfilling it! For, in so doing, you will indeed, be well on the way to living in a way which brings you personal satisfaction, imparts positive benefits to others, and therefore, proves pleasing to God. It is then that you will move into that stage in your Christian growth which BISHOP Neil Ellis delightfully describes as "walking in victory!"4

Now, it is precisely here that we come up against some of the major challenges which we inevitably encounter in our "journey of faith." For —let's face it — there will be times when we shall be called upon to combat temptations, failure in some major project, disappointment, frustration in these recessionary times, perhaps unemployment, foreclosure and debt, debilitating illness, estrangement and severe grief emanating from the death of a loved one. These are the times when questions which may test the very fabric of our faith come to the fore. Questions which have already been touched upon, which now demand our careful consideration; to whit:

"If God has determined the course of my life, in accord with His plan for it, then am I really free?"

"If I deviate from GOD's plan for my life, can I be restored to it?"

With regard to the first of these questions, it is necessary to emphasize that the Doctrine of Divine Intervention takes seriously the concept of Divine sovereignty without compromising the principle of human freedom/ responsibility. You see, while the Divine Architect has a plan for your life, and desires that you live in accord with it, He has granted you freedom to accept or reject it. For, inherent in the doctrine of creation, is the teaching that man is free, is endowed with the ability to choose good or evil. We can choose to walk in accord with the Divine Plan for our lives or we can walk away from it. Moses, towards the end of the sermons delivered to the Israelites, pointed out to the children of Israel, as they were about to cross over Jordan to enter the Promised land, that:

"I call Heaven and earth as witnesses today against you, that I have set before you life and death, blessing and cursing; therefore choose life, that both you and your descendents may live; That you may love the LORD your God, that you may obey HIS VOICE, and that you may cling to Him, for he is your life and the length of your days, and that you may dwell in the land which the Lord swore to your Fathers, to Abraham, Isaac and Jacob, to give them." Deut. 30:19-20.

According to the declaration of Moses here, God sets before us two ways, that of obedience which leads to life and that of disobedience which leads to death. And while it is crystal clear that it is the desire of the Divine Architect for us to choose the way of life, he does not infringe upon our freedom to choose whichever way we wish!

Turning to the New Testament, we see this principle in operation in the respective responses of two men, who were faced with the opportunity to follow Jesus. There was the rich young ruler who came to Jesus inquiring about discipleship. When the Master called upon him to sell his material possessions and then follow Him, he went away "sad, for he had great possessions" (Mk. 10:22) Thus, he missed the opportunity to become one of the early disciples of Jesus because he simply did not want to "give up" his material treasure. Or, as one scholar has put it, he went away sad, choosing the way of destruction not because he had great possessions, but because great possessions had him."

By contrast, the Ethiopian eunuch whom Philip the evangelist instructed, made the decision to become a disciple of Christ. After his baptism, he "went on his way rejoicing." (Acts 8:39).

Yes one said "No!" to Christ and went on his way sad. The other said "Yes" to Christ and went on his way....... glad! Jesus sums up the teaching of the Bible with this warning:

"Enter by the narrow gate; for wide is the gate and broad is the way that leads to destruction, and there are many who go in by it.

Because narrow is the gate and difficult is the way which leads to life and there are few who find it."(Matt 7:13-14)

The Divine Architect, then, who has a plan for your life and mine, while desiring that we should walk in it, does not force us to so do, leaving it up to us to choose or reject it. There is recognition of the right of the individual to choose or reject the divine plan for his/her life.

The awesome responsibility which devolves upon us in being endowed with choice by the Creator is certainly an extremely important aspect of Christian living, consistently emphasized by internationally recognized Bahamian teacher, evangelist, pastor, writer and motivator, Dr. Myles Munroe. He puts the position in these challenging words:

"Whether you use the ability God has deposited within you is totally up to you. How well you assume the responsibilities God gives you is not so much a question of how much you do, but rather how much of the available power you use. What you are doing is not near what your ability is." [5]

We come now to the second question, which logically follows that which has just been answered. It has to do with the response of the Divine Architect when we do indeed, deviate from the plan set for our lives. For, make no mistake about it, there will be times when, inadvertently or deliberately, we stray away from visions that the Divine Architect has placed in our hearts.

Yes, since we have the ability to make choices, then, by making the wrong choices, we can move away from the plan God has for our lives.

Thus, it was the plan of the Divine Architect that the first couple should live in harmony in the GARDEN OF EDEN. However, they succumbed to the temptation of the Devil, who was in the guise of a Serpent and they were expelled from the Divine Presence (Genesis 2). St. Paul records, with obvious disappointment, that Demas, a promising young disciple had left him "having loved the pleasures of this world." (II Tim. 4:10) That was the choice Demas made. And in the history of humankind over the many centuries of history, the law of God has been repeatedly transgressed. As it is declared in Scripture "For all have sinned and come short of the Glory of God."

The good news however, is that no matter how far one may go from the plan for his/her life set by the Divine Architect, there is provision for him/her to get back on track, to resume living in accord with the will of God. The person then, who has "missed the mark" for some reason, who has failed to live in accord with the plan of THE LORD for his life, has the opportunity to do better, to take definite steps to get back on track, to be reconciled with God.

Is not this the message at the very heart of the Gospel, that there is pardon for the person who repents of sin and seeks to be reconciled to God and so resumes his walk with the Lord? Is not this the assurance, the blessed assurance of Divine protection evident in the Parable of our Lord telling of a Shepherd who leaves the "ninety and nine" in the safety of the fold and goes in search of the one sheep which has strayed in the wilderness? (Luke 15: 3-7) And the one who told the Parable, was he not Himself The Good Shepherd who at Calvary laid down HIS LIFE IN ORDER TO REDEEM ALL HUMANKIND? And is this not the reason why we can joyfully sing:

> There is plentiful redemption
> In the blood that has been shed:
> There is joy for all the members
> In the sorrows of the HEAD.
>
> For the love of God is broader
> Than the measures of man's mind.
> And the heart of the Eternal
> Is most wonderfully kind? 6

Moreover, the message of redemption assures us that the Divine Architect certainly does intervene in the lives of His disciples when they stray from the plan He has set for their lives, leading them back to continue along the path of righteousness.

An extremely important truth of profound theological significance for us in this study emerges here. As we have noted, it is certainly possible for us to deviate from God's plan for our lives. When that happens, we have the choice to continue in the way that leads to destruction or to seek, by penitence to return to the path He intends for us. IT HAS TO BE EMPHASIZED HOWEVER, THAT AS THE DIVINE ARCHITECT, GOD CAN INDEED, REDEEM US, FOR HE IS THE FATHER WHO WANTS TO PUT US BACK TOGETHER AGAIN. WE ARE THEN RESTORED TO CONFORM TO THE PLAN HE HAS FOR US AND THIS CAN HAPPEN NO MATTER HOW BAD WE MIGHT HAVE "MESSED UP." THIS DOES NOT HOWEVER, ALTER THE OVERALL PLAN OF THE

GREAT ARCHITECT FOR THE LIFE OF THE INDIVIDUAL AND INDEED, FOR THE ULTIMATE PURPOSE OF HIS UNIVERSE. THIS IS THE BURDEN OF ST. PAUL'S TEACHING:
"WE KNOW THAT IN ALL THINGS GOD WORKS FOR THE GOOD OF THOSE WHO LOVE HIM, WHO ARE THE CALLED ACCORDING TO HIS PURPOSE." ROMANS 8:28 7

Interestingly then, while we may "mess up" and deviate from the plan of the Divine Architect for our life, we cannot disrupt the plan of the Divine Architect for His world. All this is well summed up in that wonderful verse of redemption assuring of the Divine Architect's concern for the welfare of each individual in the world, which he sustains and loves:
"FOR GOD SO LOVED THE WORLD THAT HE GAVE HIS ONLY BEGOTTEN SON THAT WHOSOEVER BELIEVES IN HIM SHOULD NOT PERISH: BUT HAVE ETERNAL LIFE." JOHN 3:16 8
Yes, the Divine Architect, who has a plan for the world and each individual, allows each person the freedom to depart from His will for each one's life and to return to it, while maintaining His plan for His World.

That God has a plan for the world and a purpose for the life of each and every person in it, as we have seen, is very well expressed in two verses of a hymn, which was very popular during my school days.9 And, even though it is more than half a century since I graduated, I can still recall most vividly the vigour and conviction with which we sang:

"God is working His purpose out,
As year succeeds to year;
God is working His purpose out,
And the time is drawing near-

Nearer and nearer draws the time-
The time that shall surely be,
When the earth shall be filled with
The Glory of God as the waters cover
the sea.?" 10

Dear reader, while I did not understand then why we sang this hymn with such enthusiasm, I certainly do now! You see, as thoughtful young men, studying at a Christian institution at a time when many of the "movies" we watched featured the battles of WORLD WAR II, when memories of that war were fresh in the minds of our parents and teachers, when the first generation of huge computers heralded major advances in technology, and the invention of the polio vaccine by Dr. Jonas Salk raised high hopes for a healthy world, free from this disease, which had inflicted so much suffering upon human kind, we entertained high hopes that the world would be a better place and we wanted to take our part in it. YES, WE BELIEVED THAT THE DIVINE ARCHITECT DID HAVE A PLAN AND PURPOSE WHICH HE WAS WORKING OUT IN THE COURSE OF HISTORY, AND WE WANTED TO BE A PART OF IT!

SUCCINTLY, WHILE THE OLD MEN DREAMED DREAMS OF THE GREAT WARS OF THE TWENTIETH CENTURY, WE THE YOUNG MEN, HAD VISIONS OF A BRAVE NEW WORLD IN WHICH WE WOULD HASTEN THE PACE TO BRING ABOUT A NEW ERA OF PEACE AND PROSPERITY.

Throughout this study, in which we have looked at the lives of an ancient leader and a contemporary one, Joseph and Barack Obama we have been impressed by the striking parallels between them. This study has, indeed brought out the importance of a sense of vision, determination, faith and the ability to inspire others for leadership. All this however, will mean very little unless you apply them to your own life. Yes, it can only make a difference to you if you seek, by the grace of God, to fulfill the plan of the Divine Architect for your life!

FOR YOU SEE, THE MEN AND WOMEN WHO HAVE MOST PROFOUNDLY INFLUENCED THE COURSE OF HISTORY, WHO HAVE, EXERTED THE GREATEST INFLUENCE UPON THEIR CONTEMPORARIES, WHO HAVE INDEED, BEEN MOST GREATLY ADMIRED BY THE MEMBERS OF THEIR OWN GENERATION AND GENERATIONS THAT SUCCEEDED THEM, HAVE BEEN PRECISELY THOSE LEADERS WHO HAVE HAD THE FAITH THAT INSPIRED VISIONS OF GREATNESS, THE COURAGE TO EMBARK UPON THEM AND THE TENACITY "TO GO IN THE DIRECTION OF THEIR DREAMS"

THUS, ABRAHAM, THE ESTEEMED "PATRIARCH OF THE PATRIARCHS," LEFT THE SECURITY OF LIFE IN UR HIS HOMETOWN AS AN OLD MAN, INSPIRED BY THE VISION OF A CITY THAT HAD A FOUNDATION LAID BY NONE OTHER THAN THE DIVINE ARCHITECT. JOSEPH WAS A DESPISED HEBREW, WHO ROSE RAPIDLY TO THE POST OF VICEROY OF EGYPT, INSPIRED BY HIS DREAMS AS A BOY IN CANAAN. ALEXANDER THE GREAT HAD A DREAM TO CONQUER THE WORLD AND WHEN HE HAD DONE SO EVEN AS A YOUNG MAN, WEPT BECAUSE THERE WERE NO MORE WORLDS TO CONQUER. JOHN WESLEY, WHO EVANGELISED ENGLAND IN THE EIGHTEENTH CENTURY, HAD A VISION TO CARRY THE GOSPEL TO THE WHOLE WORLD, AS ENCAPSULATED IN HIS MOTTO, "THE WORLD IS MY PARISH." WILLIAM CAREY, IN THE NINETEENTH CENTURY, WAS INSPIRED BY A VISION TO PROCLAIM THE GOSPEL IN THE NATIONS OF THE FAR EAST, AND THAT IS WHY HE COULD

MOTIVATE OTHERS WITH HIS IMMORTAL CHALLENGE, "ATTEMPT GREAT THINGS FOR CHRIST!" EXPECT GREAT THINGS FROM CHRIST!" MOTHER THERESA ESTABLISHED AN ORDER OF NUNS TO SERVE IN THE POOREST PARTS OF INDIA, INSPIRED BY A VISION TO HELP OTHERS IN THE NAME OF CHRIST. MARTIN LUTHER KING JR., THE GREAT AFRICAN – AMERICAN CIVIL RIGHTS LEADER AND NATIONAL HERO, ELECTRIFIED THE WORLD IN HIS SPEECH DELIVERED IN WASHINGTON DC IN 1963, "I HAVE A DREAM OF A TIME WHEN PEOPLE WILL BE JUDGED, NOT BY THE COLOUR OF THEIR SKIN BUT BY THE CONTENT OF THEIR CHARACTER." AND A YOUNG MAN, BORN IN HAWAII, RAISED BY HIS WHITE MOTHER AND MATERNAL GRANDPARENTS, INSPIRED BY DREAMS OF HIS ABSENTEE FATHER IN AFRICA, EMERGED TO BECOME THE FIRST AFRICAN-AMERICAN PRESIDENT OF THE UNITED STATES OF AMERICA –BARACK OBAMA!

Yes, these all proved to be great leaders because they were prepared "to move in the direction of their dreams."

Dear reader, the question that arises out of all this is certainly "What are your dreams?"

Whatever they may be, I would exhort you, like Joseph of antiquity and Obama of our own day, to go in the direction of your dreams. Yes, if you would like to live in such a way that you make a difference, that you make a positive impact upon the lives of others, then, go, go in the direction of your dreams! In order to do that, you need to cherish your dreams, to summon the courage to attain them and, trusting in God, seek to achieve them. For, as St. Paul reminds us, "I can do all things through Christ who strengthens me."

Having passed the Biblical three score and ten threshold, I have come across far too many people who have been disappointed, upset and frustrated because they have not realized their dreams. Yes, I have met old men who wept, not because they were filled with joy like those who cried on November 04, but were filled with regret, because they failed to have realized their dreams. And this does not only apply to old men and women.

Having served for several years at a correctional institution for young men, I have seen far too many of them who have fallen between the cracks because they did not take advantage of opportunities for education. Young males, who, instead of "walking in victory" to achieve their God-given potential, are instead just wallowing in defeat and lack of self esteem. It has been distressing to have to deal with young men who have turned to crime, ruining their lives and that of others, who, had they used their God – given talents might have become great leaders, brilliant scholars, had they resolutely followed their dreams. And I have met ladies, yes, young ladies, who instead of developing their skills, have turned to prostitution, resulting in teenage pregnancy and risking infection of "the virus", a popular euphemism for AIDS!

And I have come across people "in all walks of life" who have just "given up" on life because they have stopped having visions and dreaming dreams. Yes, there are those who started out with high ambitions with great dreams of success in life. But along the way, they may have faced disappointment and they have simply given up. Yes, there is nothing more pathetic than the sight of a person who has great potential, but for some reason, has just decided to "cop out."

And dear reader what of you? Are you among those who have stopped dreaming, who once had a vision and today no longer are motivated to do better? Perhaps you are amongst those who have indeed stopped dreaming. Perhaps you have faced some major disappointment – being let down by a good friend, devastated by divorce or facing economic depravity due to the loss of employment in these hard times. If so, then I would exhort you, that having read about Joseph and Obama and again drawing inspiration from them, you will begin to dream again. Go ahead and seek to fulfill your dream.

Begin to write that book which you have been thinking about for so long. Go ahead and start the business about which you have been dreaming for so long. Go in the direction of your dreams!

But do not go alone. Go trusting in the Lord. Jesus the Master, concluded HIS conversation with Nicodemus with words which are most relevant to us as we come to the end of this comparison between Joseph and Obama:

"This is the verdict: Light has come into the world, but men loved darkness instead of light because their deeds were evil. Everyone who does evil hates the light, and will not come into the light for fear that his deeds will be exposed. But whoever lives by the truth comes into the light, so that it may be seen plainly that what he has done has been done through God." (John 3::21, NIV.)

DEAR READER, I PRAY THAT REFLECTING PROFOUNDLY UPON THE ENDEAVOURS OF JOSEPH AND OBAMA, MEN OF VISION, WHO GRASPED THE OPPORTUNITIES WHICH CAME THEIR WAY, UTILIZING TO THE FULLEST THEIR GOD GIVEN TALENTS, WILL ENCOURAGE AND INDEED INSPIRE YOU TO DISCERN AND ASSIDOUSLY PURSUE THE PLAN OF THE DIVINE ARCHITECT FOR YOUR LIFE! HERE RAVI ZACHARIAS (AS ALWAYS!) HAS SOME VERY SOUND ADVICE, WELL WORTH PONDERING AS YOU REFLECT ON YOUR OWN EARTHLY PILGRIMAGE, IN ACCORD WITH THE LIGHT GIVEN TO YOU BY THE CREATOR, THE FATHER OF OUR LORD AND SAVIOUR JESUS THE CHRIST!

"When your will becomes aligned with God's will, his calling upon you has found its home. A call may not necessarily feel attractive to you, but it will tug at your soul in an inescapable way, no matter how high the cost of following it may be. We more loosely refer to as God's call.' Yes, it is His beckoning; but it is more. It is God's vital purpose in positioning you in life and giving you the vocation and context of your call to serve him with a total commitment to do the job well." 11

As we move towards the conclusion of this contribution, it is utterly imperative for you to realize that, in the final analysis, the question of ultimate importance is not whether Joseph was an historical figure, or whether the emergence of Obama to occupy the most powerful political office "in the world today" is prophetic.

NO, THE QUESTION WHICH YOU AND I MUST PRAYERFULLY ASK OURSELVES, BEFORE GOD, AS WE COME TO THE END OF THIS REFLECTION ON THE RESPECTIVE VICISSITUDES OF JOSEPH AND OBAMA, IS SIMPLY THIS:

"AM I 'WALKING IN VICTORY', LIVING DAY BY DAY IN ACCORD WITH GOD'S VISION FOR MY LIFE?"

SO, DEAR READER, IN CONCLUSION, I CAN ONLY EXHORT YOU.... GO! YES, GO IN THE DIRECTION OF YOUR DREAMS!
SO LONG AS YOU KNOW THOSE DREAMS ARE IN ACCORD WITH THE PLAN OF THE DIVINE ARCHITECT FOR YOUR LIFE!

BOOK REVIEWS

"DREAMS FROM MY FATHER"
REVIEW OF OBAMA'S FIRST BOOK. COMPULSORY READING FOR EVERY YOUNG MALE.

Are you down in the dumps and in urgent need of something to really inspire you and lift your spirits? Ever wonder how it has been possible for an African-American man to rise from relative obscurity just a few short years ago to become the President of the United States of America. Then, you simply must read "Dreams From My Father" Barack Obama's exciting, highly informative, yea inspiring story of his early life. Make no mistake about it, this book, first published in 1996, when the writer had just entered public life and in a revised, updated version in 2004, had the distinction of being a #1 New York Times bestseller. It is bound to be read, re-read and meditated upon by "people in all walks of life" for many years to come. Also, let me just share a few thoughts with you, thoughts which came to me as I read this most interesting book, by a most remarkable man.

Firstly it has to be pointed out that this book defies classification into any neat, well-known category. Yes, it has a lot of information about Obama's youthful years, but it is not an autobiography, nor can it be classified as a book of memoirs; for such books are written by old men, those who survived until their eighties and older, then look back with nostalgia to their early years. Obama, still in his forties, has yet to write his memoirs! So what is it? Well, in the introduction, Obama gives the answer – it is "a boy's search for his father and through that search, a workable meaning for life as a black American (p. xvi)." In this book then, this dynamic, already world-famous gentleman tells the story of his early life, not simply in dull narrative style, but by reflecting profoundly upon his own inner struggle to understand the circumstances of his life and to realize the purpose of his existence. It is this quality amongst others that makes this book so interesting and capable of grasping and maintaining the attention of anyone who begins to read it. Or to put it another way, once you begin to read it you simply cannot put it down until you have read its 400 pages.

Its appeal is the fact that it is extremely well – written, simple but subtle in style, direct and even provocative at times, enticing the reader to go on to the next page. At times it reads like a suspense novel, encouraging the reader to continue to see what's next. The writer's remarkable memory, attention to detail, vivid, lively descriptions of its characters and ready wit, all combine to make this book very fascinating reading.

Amazingly, there is no "table of contents" at the beginning, so it is not possible to know in advance the sequence of events in the pages ahead. Thus, if you want to know what's next in this book, you simply have to read it! "No two ways about that!"

In the section, "Origins (pp. 1-129)", the writer records the historical background of his parents. Going back several generations, he reveals that his father was a well-educated gentleman from Kenya, who travelled to Hawaii in 1959. There he met and married an ambitious white American, Stanley Ann (so named because her parents were hoping for a son), Obama's mother.

This marriage, however, did not last long. After the birth of Obama they gradually drifted apart as he returned to Kenya and his wife remained in Hawaii, eventually marrying a native islander. Thus, Obama was brought up by his mother and his maternal grand parents who were white.

This explains much about Obama. – his pride in being black, but also his concern to bring about reconciliation and thus the catchword which has become the "trademark" of his current campaign to win the nomination for the White House – CHANGE. Growing up in Hawaii and later the United States, Obama experienced the terrible effects of racism, the apathy of those blacks who seemed resigned to their "second class citizen status" and he became determined to do something about it. In his own words, Obama tells how this commitment to bring about change materialized in his mind, during his early days as a community organizer in Chicago.

"When classmates in college asked me just what it was that a community organizer did, I couldn't answer them directly. Instead I'd pronounce on the need for change. Change in the White House, where Reagan and his minions were carrying on their dirty deeds. Change in the Congress, compliant and corrupt. Change in the mood of the country, manic and self – absorbed. Change won't come from the top, I would say, change would come from mobilized grass roots. (p.133)"

Now it is most significant to point out that Obama begins his first book, not with an account of the circumstances of his birth, but with an experience as a research student, residing in New York. Just twenty-one, he was doing research in that big city, living in that unnamed, shifting border between East Harlem and the rest of Manhattan (p.3). With tremendous literary skill and consummate compassion, Obama describes the plight of an elderly black gentleman who resided on the top floor. He reveals that he would often help this old man as he struggled to lift his groceries from the basement to the top floor, stopping along the way for the old man to "catch his breath." Never a word passed between them, yet in an attitude of Christian compassion and concern for the welfare of others, Obama believed that it was his responsibility to assist this man, who never offered a word of thanks! It was not long afterwards that he died...poor, lonely and ignored by most people in that competitive metropolitan jungle!

Tears came to the eyes of this writer as he read of the death of that lonely old man. However, his admiration for Obama, already great, increased all the more because he realized that here was a man who demonstrated even in his youth, a deep concern for the welfare of the small man, the nobodies of this world, by beginning his first book with the tragic story of the passing of a lonely old black man. Such a person seemed destined for greatness!

In the pages which follow, Obama describes the early years of his life, growing up under the watchful eye of his grandparents, because his mother was occupied with her work and studies. After some years with them, he lived in Indonesia before going back to the United States. He attended high school in Los Angeles, California, at a time when the process of integration of black and white schools was in full swing. After a stint in Kenya, the home of his father, he returned to the United States, residing for a year in New York before moving to Chicago, where he spent most of his youthful years. This is why the second part of his book is devoted to his activities in "the windy city". He then returned to Kenya where he spent several eventful years learning more about the people and the customs of the birthplace of his father.

Although his father abandoned his American family when Obama was a child, Barack never forgot him. Indeed there was a constant exchange of letters between them and evidently Obama greatly valued those letters from his father - brief, direct, filled with fatherly advice! Thus, while he was raised by and spent much time with his mother, who did her best to guide him, rising early in the morning to give him extra lessons while in secondary school, he still was unable to forget his father, though estranged from him. And even after "The Old Man" (as Obama and his half brothers and sisters affectionately called him) died, young Obama was still haunted by memories of him and by thoughts of his ancestors, hence the title of the book "DREAMS FROM MY FATHER."

There can be no doubt, that a careful reading of this book is most revealing! For it enables one to understand the circumstances, experiences and impressions that combined to propel this exceptionally gifted young man to greatness. His knowledge of the background of his father, being from a small but prominent tribe in Kenya, tracing it's roots to Biblical times, certainly filled him with a sense of pride and confidence.

On the other hand, his pride in having been born in the United States of America has been demonstrated in his patriotism. Moreover, It cannot be contested, that having a White mother has contributed significantly to his wide-ranging appeal, decisively breaking down the racial barriers, which have so often soured relationships between the various ethnic bodies of the human family. This indeed, is the main reason why he has proved to be such an effective charismatic leader; able to attract people of diverse racial backgrounds. Thus he has been able to rise to prominence by appealing to and gaining the support of the vast majority of African- Americans, many young, progressive and forward – thinking young whites and a large following amongst the rapidly increasing Hispanic population

Of key significance in appreciating what makes Obama tick, is a study of his years at high school in Los Angeles. During this period he became involved in organizing groups on campus and speaking on important, "burning issues" of the day. Here is how he puts it,

" …. I found myself drawn into larger roles – contacting representatives of the African National Congress to speak on campus, drafting letters to the faculty, printing flyers, arguing strategy – I noticed that people had begun to listen to my opinions. It was a discovery that made me hungry for words. Not words to hide behind, but words that could carry a message, support an idea (p.05)."

"I noticed that people had begun to listen to my opinions!" Thus at a comparatively young age, this multi-talented gentleman realized that somehow he was gifted with the charismatic ability to draw and maintain the attention of his audience. Since those days he has gone "from strength to strength" in the competitive arena of politics, drawing huge crowds to hear him whenever and wherever he speaks. I recall a clergyman speaking about the influence of the very popular late Archdeacon William Thompson "When Willie speaks, the people listen." he observed. Likewise when Barack (which means "blessed" in Arabic as well as Hebrew) speaks, people by the thousands in his audience and millions, watching on TV screens in every corner of the globe, listen.

But there is more to it than that! Because he has already reached so far, he has elicited the attention, affection and admiration of black people everywhere. It is most significant to bear in mind and reflect profoundly upon another experience which took place early in his adult life. Obama tells of a party which went until the wee hours of the morning, by which time those who had not left had fallen asleep, most of them drunk. Just Obama and a young lady with whom he had a conversation about race earlier in the night, were still up and sober. Regi was reflecting upon her accusatory reprimand. It made Obama feel like "I was somehow responsible for the fate of the entire black race" (p.92)."

Well, it has turned out to be prophetic! For there can be not a shadow of a doubt that at this time, the attention of virtually every black person on the planet is focused upon Barack Obama as he becomes the first Black to attain the high and powerful post of President of the U.S.A. In a sense most profound, the destinies of all black people are tied to the audacious move of this African-American towards "The White House."

Recent events will certainly cause one to reflect upon Obama's religious beliefs, especially as at one stage, some claimed that he was a Muslim. Those reading the book now, will pay close attention to the second section on Chicago, in which the writer tells about his meeting with the Rev. Jeremiah Wright and eventually becoming a member of Wright's huge congregation. Moreover, it is most interesting to note, that Obama quotes a passage from the Bible at the very beginning of his book.

"For we are strangers before thee and sojourners as were all our fathers (I Chron.29:1)" These words taken from the book of Chronicles, were spoken by King David during the earthly years of his sojourn. No doubt in quoting it, Obama is conscious of his own background in being the son of an African, who lived in Hawaii before returning home, and of a white American mother, who had to be constantly on the move, due to changing circumstances with her family, the pursuit of a better life economically and in order to help the poor in the undeveloped countries of the world. But in a sense most profound, it is pertinent to us all. For we all are sojourners as we move from one place to another, from one experience to another in the pilgrimage of life!

Now if there is one thing that "shines through" in this book, it is that Barack Obama is "essentially speaking" at once a realist and an optimist! He is a man of courage, prepared "to take the bull by the horns" as he faces up to the challenges of life! It has been truly said that obstacles, setbacks and disappointments in life can make us "either bitter or better." It is crystal clear that Obama has chosen the latter! While fully aware of the challenges, attacks and setbacks of racism, there is no trace of bitterness towards the white man, nor is there any trace of self-pity, self-denigration nor despair in his writings.

That many of the young males "in the world today" are not realizing their potential, not turning their dreams into reality, failing to fulfill the plan of the Divine Architect for their lives, is a social phenomenon which disturbs the minds of leading social workers, clergypersons and politicians in the world today" This is why Obama's first, inspiring work, while it can be read with great benefit by people "in all walks of life," for young males it is a "MUST" - ABSOLUTELY!!!!!!!!!!!

Title: DREAMS FROM MY FATHER
Author: Barack Obama
Publisher: Three Rivers Press
Pages: 480
Date: August 10th, 2004
New York Times Bestseller

BOOK REVIEWS

BARACK OBAMA BARES HIS SOUL IN.......... "THE AUDACITY OF HOPE"

Those who have read and benefited from Barack Obama's first, exciting, inspiring book, DREAMS FROM MY FATHER, will most certainly be delighted to know that he has contributed a second, THE AUDACITY OF HOPE. Indeed, it is submitted that a careful reading of his first published work, is essential for an appreciation of the second.

Despite its arresting title and most attractive cover featuring a "candid photo" of the now world- famous author, the 376 page hard cover dust jacket edition can appear somewhat intimidating to all but the most avid of readers! Fortunately however, the writer presents a very useful preview of its contents in the prologue. Beginning with a very interesting description of a typical day in the life of a senator in the capital of the USA, he goes on to recount what is to come, for the benefit of the reader.

Concisely, the book falls into two parts, though it is not so indicated in its table of contents. In the first, consisting of chapters one to five, as may be expected, he deals with matters pertaining to politics and government. In the process, he gives insights into the complex processes, the interplay between "the power brokers" in the main political parties and the many conditions and forces involved in bringing about the legislation required for the operation of a democratic nation such as the USA.

While trying to be objective, Obama makes it clear that he views developments in the political arena from the perspective of one who is a Democrat. There is however, the realization that often it is necessary to co-operate even with one's political enemies in order to get certain things done. In this regard, a statement he makes about such cooperative effort, merits most careful attention, as it may give some indication as to how he may operate as President. "Commenting on this matter, Obama admits that "Occasionally, I would partner up with even my most conservative colleagues to work on a piece of legislation, and over a poker game or a beer, we might conclude that we had more in common than we publicly cared to admit." (p. 9).

The third chapter, wherein Obama deals with the Constitution of the United States, is most illuminating and noteworthy, precisely because since publishing this work, the author has been elected to serve as President of that great nation. Demonstrating vast knowledge of the historical background and operation of same, the politician expresses great admiration for it's framers and faith in its adaptability to serve as the basis for government of the "land of the free and the home of the brave." Here, it has to be pointed out that in reading this book, one is ever conscious that its author is a very gifted person, blessed with a brilliant, analytical mind, capable of assessing, processing and making wise observations on an encyclopedic amount of data. This is evident in the fact that there is not a single footnote in the entire work, which must be regarded as at once highly creative and most absorbing. As in the case of his first book, the reader is enticed to continue reading until he/she reaches the last chapter!

In the second part, Obama expresses his thinking on a number of important issues impacting on life in his native land and abroad. His View on the economy is particularly important, given the fact that it has been officially declared that the USA is "in recession." Asserting that "a nation that can't control its energy sources can't control its future," he goes on to conclude that, "Education, science and technology. Investments in these three key areas would go a long way in making America more competitive." (p.171.).

In the chapter on religion, Obama confidently makes the claim that he is a Christian (p. 223).This is noteworthy, as there are those who have questioned his allegiance to the Christian religion. On the matter of race, the author, who is of mixed racial background, expresses pride in being African – American without prejudice towards those of other racial groups. It is this tolerance, well expressed in his rallying declaration which electrified the delegates at the Democratic Party Convention in 2004, "There is not a Black America or a White America or a Latino America!" which has enabled him to appeal to and gain the support of people representing all races in the USA.

The chapter on foreign relations also merits attention, in the light of the fact that the young politician's lack of experience in that arena has been highlighted, especially by his opponents during the campaign. The book concludes with an interesting chapter in which the author reveals much about his own home and family life, confessing great love for and dependence upon his charming wife, Michelle. So, he gives this "tid bit" about his courtship. "I asked if I could kiss her. It tasted of chocolate" (p.330).Throughout this chapter, Mr. Obama "comes across" as a genuine family man, who loves his wife and their two delightful daughters and holds tenaciously to old –fashioned family values. Likewise, Michelle has always made it clear that she places high priority on the upbringing of their children, and is not prepared to compromise her attention to them, by seeking to be in the political limelight! The presence of such a family in The White House" should go a long way to positively influencing the quality of home and family life in the USA, where traditional family values are being challenged!

In this regard the book is not without its pathos, in the light of events which have transpired since it came on the market in 2006. The book is dedicated by its now highly influential writer:

"To the women who raised me – my maternal grandmother, TUTU, who's been a rock of stability throughout my life and my mother, whose loving spirit sustains me still."

Well, his mother died a few years ago after a short battle with cancer. And as is very well –known, Obama's ailing Grand Mother, for whom he interrupted his busy campaign in order to visit her in Hawaii, passed away on the eve of his election as President Elect of The USA. One cannot help being touched by the fact that the two white ladies who most deeply influenced the life of Obama during his crucial formative years, did not live to see the night of his election as the first African – American President of the USA, TUESDAY, November 4th., 2008, when old men wept and young people (of all races) rejoiced!

At the beginning of this book, the author reveals quite clearly its purpose: "how we might begin the process of changing our politics and our civic life." (p. 9). As President of the United States of America, he will be uniquely positioned to do just that!

Title: The Audacity of Hope Thoughts on Reclaiming The American Dream.
Author: BARACK OBAMA
Publisher: Crown , Division of Random House, Inc.
Pages: 376
Date: 2006 AD.
The #1 New York Times Bestseller.

PRAYER FOR BARACK OBAMA

BLESS, O LORD, WE BESEECH THEE, BARACK OBAMA AS HE ASSUMES THE OFFICE OF PRESIDENT OF THE UNITED STATES OF AMERICA.

ENDOW HIM WITH ALL THE GIFTS AND GRACES THAT HE NEEDS TO LEAD THE PEOPLE OF THE WORLD'S, MOST POWERFUL NATION DURING THE YEARS AHEAD.

GRANT HIM WISDOM THAT HE MAY BE LED TO SELECT THE BEST PERSONS TO ASSIST HIM AS HE SERVES AT THE HELM OF THIS GREAT NATION. PROTECT HIM FROM ALL HARM AND DANGER.

GRANT HIM HEALTH AND STRENGTH TO
"KEEP ON KEEPIN' ON."
GRANT HIM THE SPIRIT OF CO-OPERATION
THAT HE MAY GAIN THE SUPPORT AND AP-
PROVAL OF ALL.

BLESS HIS WIFE. MICHELLE AND THEIR TWO
DAUGHTERS.
O DIVINE ARCHITECT, BLESS YOUR SERVANT
BARACK OBAMA,

THAT HE MAY PROVE TO BE YOUR INSTRU-
MENT FOR THE BRINGING OF PEACE AND PROS-
PERITY TO THE PEOPLE OF THE UNITED STATES
OF AMERICA
AND TO ALL PEOPLE THAT ON EARTH DO
DWELL, THROUGH CHRIST WE PRAY,
AMEN.

PRAYER OF THE WRITER ON TUESDAY, NO-
VEMBER 4TH., 2008AD,
"THE NIGHT OLD MEN WEPT AND YOUNG PEO-
PLE (OF ALL RACES)..... REJOICED!"

NOTES

CHAPTER ONE

1. Conversation of the author with an old lady on Saturday Nov 07th 2008 in Freeport, Grand Bahama, Bahamas.

2. Commentators in the mainstream media concentrated on the historical aspects, while there were those who sought to evaluate same from a religious and theological perspective.

3. The Nassau Guardian, Nassau Bahamas, Thursday November 05, 2008.

4. The gentleman used Bahamian dialect. In Standard English he meant "Reverend they threw everything at him but God protected him." Essentially he expressed the opinion that despite experiencing many adversities, Obama succeeded because of Divine protection and blessing. In this regard, it is relevant to point out that the word "barach" in both Arabic and Hebrew means "blessed." More on this as our discussion proceeds in this study.

5. T.D. Jakes appeared on CNN on Tuesday November 03, 2008, the eve of Obama's historic election.

6. The discussion with the Anglican priest took place

on Saturday November 08, 2008 at a prayer conference at the pro – Cathedral of Christ the King, Freeport, Grand Bahama, Bahamas. The rector is Canon Harry Bain.

7. "In the natural" is an expression to describe the evaluation of events from a purely secular perspective. Its counterpart is the viewpoint that there are certain events which can only be described in terms of a spiritual explanation of the events of history.

8. The reference is to Genesis chapters 37, 39-50, to be discussed in detail later in this study.

9. It is often said, that every adult remembers exactly where he or she was when learning of the assassination of President John F. Kennedy. Likewise, is it too much to suggest that "every adult on planet Earth" who heard that historic announcement will always remember exactly where he/she was when it was made?

10. In order to understand what these particular locales mean to Obama, it is necessary to read his book <u>DREAMS FROM MY FATHER</u>, a review of which is included in this work.

11. This writer vividly recalls visiting a home in a "white neighborhood" while studying at a seminary in the USA back in the early 70's, when a white man referred to an elderly black man old enough to be his father as "the boy."

12. The picture of Jesse Jackson social activist, who had served with Dr. Martin King Jr. and Himself a leading advocate of Civil Rights and former candi-

date for the nomination of the Democratic Party, for the office of President, whose crying touched the hearts of many in a scene most profound of the "old men who wept" on that historic night. These included leaders such as the Rev. Dr. Joseph Lowrey, Julian Bond and J. Whitney Young

13. Considering that more than 40 years had expired since the Civil Rights Movement reached its zenith, many participants in the struggle did not live to see the election of Barack Obama.

14. Dr. Jackson Burnside was a prominent Bahamian dentist, educated in the USA at a time of strict racial segregation. Dr. Burnside was a strong advocate of social justice. This writer first saw a copy of Ebony, while as a child he visited the home of Dr. Burnside.

15. For a detailed and accurate account of the historical events referred to here, see Irving L. Jensen's SURVEY OF THE Old TESTAMENT, Chicago Moody Press 1980 5th printing pp217-241.

16. Taking into consideration that gold is currently worth hundreds of dollars per ounce, the total amount contributed must equate to millions of dollars in today's currency.

CHAPTER TWO

1. Wesley Methodist Church was established in 1847 as a result of the endeavours of English missionaries in Grant's Town, where Africans, liberated from slave ships after the abolition of the slave trade in

1807, were settled. Like many such chapels in the Caribbean, it was named in tribute to the life and teaching of John Wesley, "The Founder of Methodism under God." On the settlement of liberated Africans in the Bahamas, see the seminal work by the up-and-coming Bahamian historian, Dr. Rosanne Adderley, NEW NEGROES FROM AFRICA," BLOOMINGTON, INDIANA: INDIANA UNIVERSITY PRESS, 2006AD.

2. The "African Diaspora" is the expression used by contemporary historians and sociologists in describing the descendants of the slaves from Africa, who inhabit the southern states of the United States of America, the Islands of the Caribbean, and the nations of Central and South America.

3. "Zero tolerance" is the term used by The Royal Bahamas Police Force in its campaign to eliminate criminal activity in the Commonwealth of the Bahamas.

4. Ecclesiastes 3:1. The Psalms and Wisdom literature of the Old Testament (Proverbs, Job, and Ecclesiastes) have always proved to be favorite scripture passages of the people of The African Diaspora."

5. "Being done "is a technical expression of Latin American Liberation Theology. It has to do with the dynamic relationship between thought and action at the heart of Liberationist thinking and application of Scripture and Theology to life. The writer has discussed this aspect of liberation theology in his doctoral dissertation, "Exodus and Sinai in the Theology of Liberation: A Discussion of the Relationship Between Biblical and Marxist concepts in

Latin American Liberation Theology with special reference to the works of Gustavo Gutierrez and Jose Porfirio Miranda", presented to the University of Aberdeen, in fulfillment of the requirements of the Degree, Doctor of Philosophy, 1985 AD.

6. A favorite saying of the writer. This famous statement of the great African educator is a motto of the Bethany Bible and Training Institute Freeport, Grand Bahama.

7. The Rev. Dr. Daniel Antwi is now a professor at a seminary in Accra, Ghana.

8. On socio-economic conditions in the Bahamas during the decades leading up to Independence in 1973, see Dr. Doris Johnson's "THE QUIET REVOLUTION," Nassau 1976.

9. "For the people" was the expression used to describe the aspirations and struggles of the black majority of the Bahamas during the years leading up to Independence. The writer discusses this matter in his book Let Us Build A Christian Nation, Freeport Bahamas 2004 AD, pp, 20-37.

10. Psalm 68 as will be demonstrated, is a favorite text of the advocates of black theological and religious movements in the USA and the Caribbean.

11. This oft quoted passage comes from the famous "I HAVE A DREAM SPEECH" of Dr. Martin Luther King Jr.

12. See "Washington, Booker Taliaferro" in Colliers Encyclopedia Vol.23, New York: McMillan Educa-

tional Company 1994, p281.

13. According to Uncle Charlie, Daniel Emmett Scott worked closely with Booker T. Washington. He named my father Emmett, a name which has come down our family line, showing the deep influence of the ideas of Booker T. Washington upon it.

14. My siblings include Mrs. Miriam Curling, Attorney at Law, who resides with her family in Nassau: Dr. Roger Leslie Weir, a professor in neuropharmachology at Howard University Hospital Washington DC. And Ms. Sheila Weir, a retired teacher, who resides with her family in Atlanta, Georgia.

15. See address by Barack Obama in USA Today, Monday November 10 2008AD.

16. See the review of Obama's book <u>DREAMS FROM MY FATHER,</u> Three Rivers Press, 2004

17. Exposition of this text will be carried out throughout this contribution.

CHAPTER THREE

1. Expression coined by a Bahamian gentleman to describe the sense of urgency of the present generation. Based on the fact that today many use the microwave to prepare meals in minutes, something which often took our parents hours of laborious cooking on gas or electric stoves. The writer uses this expression in another work, <u>"PRAYING THROUGH THE POWER OF PERSISTENCE IN PRAYER."</u> the writer's unpublished manuscript.

2. Alvin Toffler, <u>FUTURE SHOCK</u> Bantam June 1, 1984 The writer vividly recalls that while he was a theological student in the United States during 1970–71, this book was the main topic of discussion at seminars, with constant references being made to it from the pulpit. Everyone was excited about the new changes taking place as a result of advances in technology.

3. Observation made by the Rev. Derek C.O. Browne during devotional period at a meeting held on Thursday November 20th., 2008 at Wesley Methodist Church (MCCA),Nassau, Bahamas. The Rev. Mr. Browne is a Minister of the Methodist Church in the Caribbean & THE Americas.

4. The writer was born and spent the formative years of his life when the Commonwealth of the Bahamas was a colony of the British Empire, as were all the countries of the English speaking Caribbean. Most of them have since become independent nations. The Bahamas became independent on July 10, 1973.

5. A certain American business executive, himself a golfer, opined that golfers would always be white, while caddies would always be black.

6. It is amazing how few people outside the USA had heard anything about Barack Obama before he announced his intention to seek the nomination of the Democratic Party as a candidate for the Presidency of the USA.

7. The writer recalls being deeply impressed by the Illinois Senator when first seeing him on a television

program in 2007.

8. See Introductory Chapter, "The Night Old Men Wept, and Young People (of all races!) Rejoiced!"

9. The writer demonstrated that the Exodus has proved to be a source of inspiration to oppressed people in their struggle for social justice (especially the poor of the Third World) in his dissertation, "EXODUS AND SINAI IN THE THEOLOGY OF LIBERATION: A DISCUSSION OF THE RELATIONSHIP BETWEEN BIBLICAL AND MARXIST CONCEPTS IN LATIN AMERICAN LIBERATION THEOLOGY WITH SPECIAL REFERENCE TO THE WORKS OF JOSE PORFIRIO MIRANDA AND GUSTAVO GUTIERREZ," presented to the University of Aberdeen in fulfillment of the requirements for the Degree Doctor Of Philosophy,1985. The Thesis – that the Bible takes priority over Marxism – was sustained.

10. See the writer's, <u>LET US BUILD A CHRISTIAN NATION,</u> Freeport, Grand Bahama, Bahamas, 2006.

11. On the major contribution of this great scholar see "Gerhard von Rad: "Theologian of the Church." In interpretation, Volume 62 Number 3 July 2008, Union Theological Seminary Presbyterian School of Christian Education, Richmond, Virginia, USA.

12. Gerhard von Rad, <u>Genesis,</u> ET, London: SCM Press, 1972 (Revised Ed.), pp.347.

13. Rendering in an early translation in English.

14. See Merriam – Websters Collegiate Dictionary's 11th Edition definition of "Hebrew" Page 576

15. von Rad, ibid., p. 368. Evidently, the "Hebrews originally were a wandering group of people, belonging to no particular nationality or tribe, comparable in many respects to modern gypsies.

16. Scholars date the rule of Joseph in Egypt to about 1800 BC., during the dynasty of the Hyskos who were, on the whole, generous in their attitude to nomadic tribes such as the Hebrews. See Irving L. Jensen, Jensen's Survey Of The Old Testament, Chicago Moody Bible Institute, 1980, pp.63 – 80.

17. The Egyptian name given to Joseph by Pharaoh on his appointment as viceroy.

18. (Gen. 41-45). Joseph has been styled as "Prime Minister," "Governor" and other terms to describe delegated authority. The title preferred here is "Viceroy." DEFINED as "The governor of a country or province who rules as representative of the sovereign." (Miriam- Webster Dictionary, Springfield, Illinois, USA.).

19. The Rev. Joseph Lowrey, prominent leader in the Civil Rights Movement preached a sermon on this text, highlighting the need to be alert to opportunities to engage in the struggle for social justice for the oppressed at Wesley Methodist Church. Nassau, Bahamas, in the summer of 1990.

20. The Hyksos, who were favorable to the Hebrews were deposed about 1570 BC, being replaced by a new dynasty which was not nearly as amicably dis-

posed to them. See Jensen, ibid., p. 84.

21. Editorial in "USA TODAY," Thursday November 6, 2008, p. 11A.

22. See. "Ebony" Magazine for November 2008.

23. Barack Obama, <u>Dreams From My Father</u>, P. 92.

24. See Chapter Two, "Lessons From Aunt Lily."

25. See "The Liberationist Trend Christianity Conceived as a Black Man's Religion", in the writer's <u>LET US BUILD A CHRISTIAN NATION,</u>.

26. On the struggle for racial and social justice in the USA, see the survey by Cornell West, <u>Prophecy Deliverance: An Afro –American Revolutionary Crisis</u>, Maryknoll, NY; Orbis Books, 1990. On the struggle for racial and social justice in the Caribbean see Kortright Davis, <u>"Emancipation Still Comin.</u>" <u>Explorations in Caribbean Emancipatory Theology,</u> Maryknoll, NY: Orbis Book, 1990

27. See Chapter One, "The Night Old Black Men Wept...... And Young People (of All Races) Rejoiced.

28. In discussing the contribution of Booker T. Washington with some persons both in the USA and the Caribbean, the writer has found that there were those who regarded him as "Uncle Tom." Early during the campaign of Obama, there were those opposed to him, who identified themselves as "Blacks Against Obama!"

29. See, Booker T. Washington, in Collier's Encyclopedia, Vol. 23, p. 282.

30. Washington lived at a time when racial segregation was still prevalent and Blacks were "second class citizens." As such, it was inconceivable that a BLACK MAN could even countenance seeking the office of President of the USA.

31. The writer, who is old enough to remember the events of the Civil Rights Movements in the mid-twentieth century, has been most deeply impressed by the confident manner in which Obama spoke about his decision to "run" for the office of President of the USA! To him it seemed unbelievable!

CHAPTER FOUR

1. This matter will be discussed in detail in the next chapter.

2. On the historicity of the Joseph Narrative and the Exodus, see the NIV Archaeological Study Bible, Grand Rapids; Zondervan, 2006.

3. The writer has dealt with Joseph's actions here in the article (unpublished) "Why Joseph Never Wrote a Book."

4. Here Matthew, who always sought to demonstrate the fulfillment of the prophesies of the Old Testament in the New, quotes a text of Hosea 11:1.

5. The unique ministry of Philip has been dealt with

by the writer in the unpublished article, "Philip the Deacon, Who Became an Evangelist."

6. See <u>The Pulpit Commentary</u> Vol. 18 p. 274.

7. Edward W. Blyden, <u>Christianity, Islam and The Negro Race,</u> Baltimore, MD: Black Classic Press, 1994 (First published 1888), p.188. Blyden, a native of St. Thomas, US Virgin Islands, was one of the pioneer scholars to emerge from the Third World.

8. Sam Wellman. <u>David Livingstone Missionary and Explorer,</u> RICHVILLE, OHIO – Barbour Publishing Inc., ND., P.204.

9. The President of the World Council of Churches is the Rev. Dr. Samuel Kobia.

10. The writer embarked upon theological studies as a lay preacher in the early fifties, entering seminary in Kingston, Jamaica in 1959 and remaining until 1963. More than 90% of the text books used or recommended were published in the nations of the North Atlantic, with precious few coming from the Caribbean, or the wider Third world.

11. The writer has discussed this matter in detail in his doctoral dissertation.

12. See Noel l. Erskine, <u>Decolonizing Theology: A Caribbean Perspective,</u> Maryknoll, NY; Orbis Books, 1983 and William Watty, <u>From Shore To Shore,</u> Kingston Jamaica, 1981. The Rev. William Watty served as President of the United Theological College of the West, Kingston Jamaica.

13. The writer has made two trips to Korea and on each

occasion was astonished and encouraged by the rapid growth and spiritual depth of the Churches. It has several of the largest congregations in the world. More than 700 missionaries from Korea are serving in foreign lands, mainly in Asia. See, The Korean Methodist Church., Seoul, Korea, 2006 AD

14. See Jose Comblin, The Meaning of Mission, ET, Dublin: Gill & MacMillan Ltd., 1979 and Tim Codner, The Church in Transition, Grand Rapids: Zondervan, 2006

15. See Walbert Buhlmann, The Coming of The Third Church,, Slough England: St. Paul Publications 1976. See also Colleen Birchett, England: St. Paul Publications.

16. See Buhlmann, pp. 80 -154, especially "Africa's Hour."

17. The writer recalls an English missionary early in the 1950s predicting that the time would soon come for missions to become "a two way street" At that time, virtually all mission activity in the denomination concerned was indeed, a "one way street" – missionaries coming to The Third World from the developed nations of The North Atlantic, with very few moving in the opposite direction!

18. Joseph was greatly admired by my peers during those youthful years when most males look for role models to inspire them in their endeavors.

19. Several scholars, including Gerhad von Rad, have put forward the thesis that "The Joseph Narrative" should be classified as Wisdom Literature," like

Proverbs, Job and Ecclesiastes, because of its strong Wisdom motifs. There is much to commend this view. On Wisdom Literature, see the writer's "Theodicy Israel and the Ancient Near East," presented to Christian Theological Seminary, in partial fulfillment of the requirements for the Master of Sacred Theology Degree.

20. In the days before the signing of Magna Carta in 1215, monarchs ruled with absolute power, without the "checks and balances" of our time.

21. It is interesting to note that Joseph came to power at the age of thirty, considerably younger than Obama, who won the race for the White House at the age of 48 on the night when old Black men wept and young people of all races rejoiced!

CHAPTER FIVE

1. See B.K. Kuiper, The Church In History, Grand Rapids, Michigan: Eerdmans Publishing Co.,, 1994, p.39.

2. On Deism see Kuiper, p. 302.

3. See Ravi Zacharias, The End of Reason A Response to The New Atheists, Grand Rapids, Michigan: Zondervan, 2008 AD.

4. Based on discussions with an architect with a view to the construction of a residence in Nassau, Bahamas.

5. See Suzanne de Dietrich, ET God's Unfolding Purpose, Philadelphia: The Westminister Press, 1957

and /or Finis Jennings Dake, <u>God's Plan For Man The Key To The World's Storehouse of Wisdom</u>, LAURENCEVILLE, Georgia: Dake Bible Studies, 1977

6. See Myles Munroe, <u>Understanding Your Potential</u> with a foreword by Dr. Jerry Horner, Shippingberg, PA: Destiny, 1991.

7. On the life and contributions of this outstanding Caribbean churchman see, Yvonne O. Coke, <u>Eternal Father, Bless Our Land,</u> Kingston, Jamaica: LMH Publishing, 2000AD.

8. Von Rad, p. 14.

9. Derek Kidner, <u>Genesis An Introduction and Commentary,</u> Leister, England: Inter – Varsity Press, 1967, 180.

10. Kidner, p. 191.

11. On the precarious nature of the daily living of the inhabitants of the countries of the Middle East at the time of the Patriarchs, see the article, "Famine in the Ancient Near East," in <u>The Archaeological Study Bible</u> Grand Rapids: Zondervan, 2005AD., p. 70.

12. It is suggested that the rendering of this text in the NIV brings out its essential meaning as indicative of God's working out of all events, through the vicissitudes of human kind, in accordance with His plan.

CHAPTER SIX

1. On this school of theology see Dake, God's Plan For Man, pp.3-9.

2. See Obama's first exciting book, Dreams From My Father, which is reviewed in this contribution.

3. See BARACK OBAMA, The Audacity of Hope, New York: Crown Publishers (Random House), 2006 AD., "Politics,"pp.101 -135.

4. Norman Vincent Peale served for many years as Pastor of Marble Collegiate Church in New York, He believed in positive thinking and wrote the best-seller, The Power of Positive Thinking.

5. Cardinal Sheen was a pioneer in the field of Christian Communications. He produced the TV program "LIFE IS WORTH LIVING" back in the fifties, when religious TV programming was in its infancy.

6. Dr. Myles Munroe, in many of his sermons, articles and books, has emphasized the importance of having a sense of purpose, for success in life.

7. See T. D. Jakes' book, **REPOSITION YOURSELF LIVING LIFE WITHOUT LIMITS**, NEW YORK: New York: ATRIA Books, 2007 AD

8. Joyce Meyer, "Enjoy Your Life" Program on TBN, Tuesday, December 02., 2008 AD.

9. Bishop Neil Ellis is the PASTOR of Mt. Tabor Full Gospel Baptist Church, Nassau, Bahamas. A positive theme, emphasizing the call of the Christian "to

walk in victory," pervades his sermons and published works.

10. Dr. Rodney Smothers a minister of the United Church. Powerful preacher and Evangelist, He stresses the need for commitment to Christ.

11. Dr. Yvonne Capehart, <u>DRAWN TO DESTINY How to Discover and Bring to Fruition Your True Purpose in Life</u>, Denver, Colorado: Legacy Publishers Int., 2005.

12. Joel Osteen, <u>Become A Better You 7 Keys To Improving Your Life Every Day</u>, New York: Free Press, 2007 AD

13. Rick Warren, <u>The Purpose Driven Life</u> Zondervan March 17th 2007

14. Professor Paul Tillich observed that the history of humankind may be divided into three main periods, according to human phobias, "fears." Ancient man, he claimed was dominated by the fear of death, medieval man was dominated by the fear of sin and modern man is dominated by the fear of meaninglessness.

CHAPTER SEVEN

1. The Rev. Dr. Nymphas Edwards is a Methodist Minister from the Caribbean, who is now serving in California, USA.

2. See the writer's article "What You Don't Use You Lose," published in "The FREEPORT News,"

Freeport, Grand Bahama, Bahamas, on Monday, November 24th., 2008.

3. The Rev. Dr. Clifton Niles made this observation while preaching a sermon at the anniversary service of St. Paul's Methodist Church, Freeport, Grand Bahama, on Sunday, October 19th, 2008.

4. "Walking in Victory" is a TV program produced by Bishop Neil Ellis. It is telecast every Sunday afternoon on ZNS-TV, Nassau, Bahamas.

5. Myles Munroe, <u>Understanding Your Potential,</u> Shippensburg, PA: Destiny IMAGE Publishers, 1991, p.72.

6. Hymn 318 in the <u>Methodist Hymnbook</u>, London: The Epworth Press, Author, Frederick William Faber (1814-'63).

7. It is suggested that the rendering of this verse in the NIV. very accurately conveys the meaning of the original Greek text.

8. It is submitted that this seminal text, sometimes called "The Bible in miniature" sums up the teaching here, that the love of God is eternal in extent, universal in scope and directed to the salvation of all humankind.

9. The writer attended Calabar High School, Kingston Jamaica, from 1955 –56. It is a well – recognized institution of secondary education, operated by the Jamaica Baptist Union.

10. <u>The Methodist Hymn Book</u>, Hymn 812, verses 1,3.

Written by Arthur Campbell Ainger (1841-1919).

11. Ravi Zacharias, <u>The Grand Weaver</u>, Grand Rapids, Michigan; Zondervan Publishing Co., 2007 AD. Ravi Zacharias is an internationally recognized and very influential contemporary Christian "apologist" As such, he is deeply involved in the intellectual defence of the Christian faith, A native of India, he resides with his family in Georgia, USA.

SELECT BIBLIOGRAPHY

PUBLISHED WORKS

Adderley, Rosanne, <u>New Negroes From Africa</u>
Bloomington, Indiana: Indiana University Press, 2006AD

Blyden, Edward W., <u>Christianity, Islam & The Negro Race</u>
Baltimore, MD.: Black Classic Press,1994
(2nd. ED. First published 1888 AD.)

Buhlmann, Walbert, <u>The Coming Of The Third Church,</u>
Slough, England: St. Paul Publications, 1976

Capehart, Yvonne, <u>Drawn To Destiny,</u>
Colorado:Legacy Pub. Intl., 2005AD

Coke, Yvonne, <u>Eternal Father Bless Our Land,</u>
Kingston, Jamaica; LMH Publishing, 2000AD.

Dake,Finis Jennings, <u>God's Plan For Man.,</u> Laurenceville, GA.;
Dake Bible Studies, 1977.

Davis, Kotright, <u>Emancipation Still Comin',</u>
Maryknoll, NY: Orbis Books, 1990 AD.

Dietrich, Suzanne, God's Unfolding Purpose.,
ET Philadelphia; The Westminister Press, 1957AD.

Erskine, Noel L., Decolonizing Theology; A Caribbean Perspective,
Maryknoll, NY Orbis Books, 1983

Jakes, T.D., Reposition Yourself, New York: Atria Books, 2007AD.

Jensen, Irving L. Survey of The Old Testament,
Chicago: Moody Bible Institute, 1980.

Kidner, Derek, Genesis An Introduction And Commentary,
Leister, England: Inter – Varsity Press, 1967AD.

Kuiper, B.K., The Church In History, Grand Rapids, Michigan, Eerdmans Publishing Co., 1994.

Munroe, Myles, Understanding Your Potential,
Shippensburg, PA.: Destiny Image Publishers, 1991 AD.

Obama, Barack, Dreams From My Father, Three Rivers Press, 2004
1994, Revised 2004 AD.

Obama, Barack, The Audacity of Hope, New York: Crown Publishers, 2006AD.

Tillich, Paul, The Courage To Be, Yale University Press, 2000 AD.

von Rad, Gerhard, Genesis, ET London: SCM Press, 1972.

Watty, William W., From Shore To Shore, Kingston, Jamaica, 1981.

Weir, J. Emmette, Let Us Build A Christian Nation, Freeport, Grand Bahama, Bahamas, 2006AD.

West, Cornell, Prophecy Deliverance., Maryknoll, NY: Orbis, 1989.

Zacharias, Ravi, The Grand Weaver, Grand Rapids, Michigan: Zondervan, 2007AD.

UNPUBLISHED WORKS

Weir, J. Emmette, "Exodus and Sinai In The Theology of Liberation:
A Discussion of The Relationship Between Biblical and Marxist Concepts in Liberation Theology With Special Reference to The Works of Jose Porfirio Miranda and Gustavo Gutierrez." Dissertation presented to the University of Aberdeen in fulfillment of requirements for the award of the Degree Doctor of Philosophy,1985.

Weir, J. Emmette, "Philip, The Deacon Who Became An Evangelist."
Freeport, Grand Bahama, Bahamas. 2008AD.

Printed in the United States
214695BV00001B/34/P